ROUTLEDGE LIBRARY EDITIONS: THE MEDIEVAL WORLD

Volume 20

FROM ROMAN EMPIRE TO RENAISSANCE EUROPE

FROM ROMAN EMPIRE TO RENAISSANCE EUROPE

DENYS HAY

Routledge
Taylor & Francis Group

LONDON AND NEW YORK

First published in 1953 by Methuen & Co Ltd

This edition first published in 2020
by Routledge
2 Park Square, Milton Park, Abingdon, Oxon OX14 4RN

and by Routledge
52 Vanderbilt Avenue, New York, NY 10017

Routledge is an imprint of the Taylor & Francis Group, an informa business

© 1953 Denys Hay

All rights reserved. No part of this book may be reprinted or reproduced or utilised in any form or by any electronic, mechanical, or other means, now known or hereafter invented, including photocopying and recording, or in any information storage or retrieval system, without permission in writing from the publishers.

Trademark notice: Product or corporate names may be trademarks or registered trademarks, and are used only for identification and explanation without intent to infringe.

British Library Cataloguing in Publication Data
A catalogue record for this book is available from the British Library

ISBN: 978-0-367-22090-7 (Set)
ISBN: 978-0-429-27322-3 (Set) (ebk)
ISBN: 978-0-367-18169-7 (Volume 20) (hbk)
ISBN: 978-0-367-18175-8 (Volume 20) (pbk)
ISBN: 978-0-429-05991-9 (Volume 20) (ebk)

Publisher's Note
The publisher has gone to great lengths to ensure the quality of this reprint but points out that some imperfections in the original copies may be apparent.

Disclaimer
The publisher has made every effort to trace copyright holders and would welcome correspondence from those they have been unable to trace.

HOME STUDY BOOKS
General Editor: B. Ifor Evans

FROM ROMAN EMPIRE TO RENAISSANCE EUROPE

by

DENYS HAY

METHUEN & CO LTD, LONDON
36 Essex Street, Strand, WC2

First published in 1953

CATALOGUE NO. 4466/U

*Printed in Great Britain by
Jarrold and Sons Ltd
Norwich*

PREFACE

IT has been my aim in this book to convey a general impression of the changes in European society during a thousand years of its development. The reader will observe that in this millennium I distinguish three epochs, each of which seems to me to possess a coherence of its own. These are: from about A.D. 300 (to speak in round numbers) to about 800; from 800 to about 1300; and from 1300 onwards to a terminus, perhaps about 1700, well beyond the close of the fifteenth century, the point at which this book ends. Though they may be justified, these divisions are in the last analysis quite arbitrary. Like all 'periods', which are merely names given to portions of the past, these are firmly mortised to each other. But if Time is indivisible it is also, in Bacon's phrase, 'the author of authors'. One cannot reflect on or write about history without arranging it in patterns.

With the first era I do no more than indicate its influence in the formation of the next. With the last, I only sketch its emergence from the preceding one. And in dealing with the central period itself, the 'middle ages' most truly so called, I have only been able to indicate very briefly a few of the great preoccupations and programmes that absorbed the attention of contemporaries. I had no room for a multiplicity of illustrative examples. My slender anthology of instances seldom draws on the rich resources of literature, architecture and the decorative arts, while specifically English material has been deliberately kept to a minimum. I can only hope that many readers will feel, as I do, an urgent inclination to read big books on big subjects and will turn to some of the works listed at the end of this volume.

The books I mention there do not represent fully my own indebtedness to others, for I have excluded periodical literature and works in foreign languages. I have, moreover, derived many notions and much information (both sought and unsought) from teachers, colleagues, and students. Even were I still able to identify what precisely I owe to these helpers, I would not attempt to name them all here. But I shall venture to thank my wife. To her and to my children I wish informally to dedicate this essay.

Besides providing a few titles of 'secondary authorities', as historians humbly refer to their own compositions, I have added a selection of original sources available in translation. What historians do should not seem mysterious. Much of their raw material may be in archaic languages or in documents which require skilled interpretation. But there is a mass of evidence which anyone can consult. The hall-mark of the historically minded person is an itch for the concrete, a desire to get behind generalizations to the facts upon which they are based and to establish an almost physical relationship with the texture of earlier times. To those who contemplate enlarging their experience through historical study I can promise a deepening sense of the reasonableness of the human past and thus a certain confidence in the future.

Edinburgh, August 1952

CONTENTS

CHAPTER	PAGE
PREFACE	v

PART I
FROM EMPIRE TO CHRISTENDOM

I. ROMAN SURVIVALS   1
Europe, Christendom, Rome, p. 1; rise and character of Roman Empire, p. 2; its disintegration, p. 4; survival of Romance language, p. 8; and of Christian religion, p. 9.

II. THE MIGRATIONS AND SETTLEMENT OF THE BARBARIANS   14
Reasons for barbarian pressure on the Empire, p. 14; the settlements, p. 18; barbarians accept and emulate the Empire, p. 21; Greek Church centred on Byzantine Emperor, p. 25; Latin Church on Bishop of Rome, p. 26; nature of barbarian kingdoms, p. 28; the last invasions, p. 33.

PART II
MANOR, FEOF, AND CHURCH

III. THE STRUCTURE OF SOCIETY   39
Geography and population of the European area c. A.D. 800, p. 39; patterns of agrarian activity, p. 42; the feudal relationship, p. 45; knights, peasants, and changes on the manor, p. 55; the clergy identified with feudal society, despite monastic reforms, p. 63; literature, learning, universities, p. 72; the 'Great Chain of Being', p. 76.

IV. LAW AND GOVERNMENT: THE CUSTODY OF CHRISTENDOM   79
Survival of Roman influences, p. 79; but triumph of customary law, p. 80; and survival of kingship, p. 82; the German Emperor and the Church, p. 90; Church reform and papal leadership, p. 91; Gregory VII and investiture, p. 98; imperium and sacerdotium, growth of papal claims, p. 100; the unity of Christendom, p. 105.

viii ROMAN EMPIRE TO RENAISSANCE EUROPE

CHAPTER	PAGE
V. BARONS, BISHOPS, AND KINGS	109

Public affairs prior to the thirteenth century narrowly localized, p. *109; the magnates' aim: to equate land with government*, p. *110; the problems of a baron*, p. *111; the enlargement of territorial lordship*, p. *118; warfare and religion*, p. *120; the First Crusade*, p. *126; German expansion*, p. *131; kings and the feudality*, p. *133; the closing of an epoch*, p. *146.*

PART III
FROM CHRISTENDOM TO EUROPE

VI. THE TOWNS	147

Development of commerce, p. *147; political and social development of the towns*, p. *152; town politics in Italy*, p. *160; Hanseatic League*, p. *167; Swiss Confederation*, p. *169; general social consequences of commerce*, p. *171.*

VII. KINGS AND COUNCILS	176

Papal sovereignty in theory and practice, p. *176; secular monarchy*, p. *179; reaction against monarchy: in the Church, the Schism and the Councils*, p. *185; the Hundred Years War and civil war*, p. *190; kings and princes emerge supreme*, p. *195; decline and overthrow of the Eastern Empire*, p. *199; the later Crusades*, p. *202.*

VIII. NEW WORLDS—ANCIENT AND MODERN	207

Intellectual and emotional innovations: (a) heresy, p. *207; (b) Mendicant Orders, Franciscans and Dominicans*, p. *210; (c) Aristotle, Averroism, and Nominalism*, p. *212; northern mysticism*, p. *216; and Italian humanism*, p. *217; concept of the 'middle age'*, p. *225; overseas exploration and the Portuguese*, p. *226; Christendom and Europe*, p. *229.*

SHORT READING LIST	233
INDEX	237

MAPS

I. EUROPE, 400 A.D.–800 A.D.	15
II. EUROPE, XIV–XV CENTURIES	193

Part I   *From Empire to Christendom*

CHAPTER I

ROMAN SURVIVALS

Empire, Christendom, Rome; rise and character of Roman Empire; its disintegration; survival of Romance language; and of Christian religion.

THE title of this book might have been 'Medieval Europe'. This has been avoided for several reasons and not least because the phrase is misleading. For almost the whole of the period covered here it is incorrect to use the terms 'Europe' and 'European'. The men and women who lived in the area we·now call Europe used a different word on the rare occasions when they wished to refer to the limits of a society larger than their village or parish, county or diocese, or kingdom. They described themselves as 'inhabitants of Christendom'. There are, moreover, practical difficulties in equating medieval Christendom with modern Europe. The two areas were not coterminous, for Christendom included large parts of Asia Minor, while Europe today includes parts of Germany and the Slav lands farther east which only came properly into Christendom at the end of the fourteenth century. Only one other concept existed as a rival to the notion of Christendom: that of the Empire. Yet that was always a weak competitor, for during the Middle Ages there were always two Empires, one in the East and one in the West, and in neither did all princes acknowledge themselves to be subjects of the emperors. The universal acceptance of Christendom as an inclusive term was not, of course, true of the second and third centuries, and we shall see that in the fifteenth century it was already ceasing to be entirely appropriate.

In the second and third centuries the broadest unit was still the Roman Empire. From the Atlantic seaboard of Spain and Gaul to the Black Sea, from the Tyne, the Rhine, and the Danube in the North to the Sahara in the South, the provincial organization of the Roman Empire stood intact and hundreds of cities reproduced in miniature the life of the City itself, Rome. So unalterable did this situation seem to contemporaries that the final overthrow of the old way of life has naturally tended to be regarded by later historians as a catastrophic event in which the defences of the Empire, maintained for so many centuries, suddenly collapsed under the overwhelming pressure of the barbarians from Germany and the central Asian plains. In fact the Romans of the third century deluded themselves. The outward structure of their society was to some extent preserved, its inward spirit was already dead. The wonder is not that that Empire finally disappeared but that it managed to survive for so long.

The farming communities of central Italy, banded together under the leadership of Rome, had, in the third and second centuries B.C., conquered the whole of the Italian peninsula and the Mediterranean littoral. Often booty had been a prime motive—the tangible wealth of captured weapons, precious metals, slaves. These commodities were poured into Rome itself and the other great towns of Italy and as the domination of Roman armies was extended, the newly conquered provinces were usually organized administratively round colonial cities modelled on the mother city of Rome. In the first century B.C. the pace of conquest slackened; groups of Roman citizens in Italy itself conspired to monopolize the dwindling income of war; and civil disturbances broke out which were only ended by a weary resignation of power into the hands of one man. Thus the Empire or Imperium, the extraordinary delegation of all power to an omnipotent military magistrate, was superimposed on the old republican forms. The Senate, for long the supreme authority in the State, gradually dwindled in importance as the Emperor and his companions controlled the army, the provinces, and the City itself.

The inhabitants of Italy and especially of Rome were entirely dependent on the issue of the simple rations of the South: bread, oil, wine. This became the principal concern of the State. The provinces themselves were equally parasitic, their towns existing mainly as centres of administration and tax collection. The taxes were gradually collected with less efficiency and more corruption; money payments became discarded in favour of payments in kind; and, although the currency was successfully reformed in A.D. 296, there was a marked reduction in the circulation of money in the following century, and an attempt to fix maximum prices was a total failure. These developments would, of course, have been fatal for a commercial, let alone an industrial, economy. But Rome had never known either. Commerce was largely concerned with luxuries and was in the hands of Syrian and Jewish merchants. Land was occasionally exploited in big estates (the *latifundia*) worked—very inefficiently—by slaves; but only a handful of great landowners regarded their estates as economic enterprises and in any case the supply of slaves dried up with the end of aggressive war. Most telling fact of all: for the Roman, a business man meant above all a money-lender and it would not be far from the truth to say that the only lively commercial activity was usury. The great highway of the Mediterranean was thus not thronged by a Roman merchant navy. The Roman roads, which are often such marvels of engineering skill, are quoted as evidence of Roman grandeur; but in fact they are pathetic monuments to a society which knew little real trade, whose towns were arbitrarily established as units in an administrative hierarchy, joined together by a network of predominantly military communications.

As the impetus of aggressive war slackened it became harder and harder to maintain the coherence of the Empire. The army, whose supremacy in politics was inevitable in a society orientated to war, made and unmade emperors, but was soon itself a feeble military instrument. The borders were protected by enlisting the barbarous and semi-barbarous tribes on the frontiers and the regular forces were concentrated for garrison duties in the vulnerable towns. Paid now, like everyone else, in doles of flour and wine, the 'Roman' soldier was usually not Roman or even Italian by descent and the outlandish origin of some of the emperors, several of whom came from the mountains of Dalmatia, bears witness to the change in the one binding force within the Empire, the army. Some of these general-emperors were remarkable men: Gallienus, Aurelianus, above all Diocletian. But their attitude to the decrepit society they were called upon to govern was essentially military. The militarization of the Empire was in any event a congenial solution to a Roman and the steps which were taken, harsh though they were, seem to have excited no active resistance. The Empire itself was divided into two great sections, the western half centred on Rome and the eastern half (after Constantine) on Constantinople: the dividing line, first made in A.D. 293, but not permanent until 364, ran north and south to the east of the heel of Italy: Illyria was in the western Empire, the Greek provinces in the eastern, Tripoli in Africa went to the western Empire, and Libya and Egypt to the eastern. In a sense this merely recognized the need to divide the defences of a vast area; but it equally pointed to a tendency for each province to become a self-sufficient entity; and, by doubling imperial establishments, it created another drain on the depleted income of the State.

For the emperors were by the third century behaving less like Roman magistrates and more like Oriental kings. The subtle compromise devised by Augustus, the first emperor, which maintained the old republican forms and concealed the authority of the first citizen (*princeps*), was abandoned by Diocletian and his successors. Their courts were now inflated in numbers and the courtiers were ranged in hierarchies of dignity according to their proximity to the imperial person. The old *cursus honorum*, the promotion of the rich public-spirited citizen through the ranks of the magistracy, was dead even in Rome, where the emperors scarcely ever resided in the third and fourth centuries; and in provincial cities the exercise of public office was an affliction, a *corvée*, for which candidates could only be found by making it an hereditary obligation. This creation of hereditary obligations was, in fact, the device adopted for solving all social problems. First the workers in State mines and factories, then the shippers of the vital supplies of Rome, then the bakers, the building workers, timber merchants, all were rigorously enlisted in guilds and subjected to hereditary discipline and compulsion. Even the pleasures of the town—and every third day in Rome was a holiday—became an inherited charge on the families of the performers, actors, musicians, gladiators. Above all, in the great estates which supported the wealthy, as exploitation by slaves gradually declined, the master was compelled to let out his land to tenant farmers, the *coloni*. These *coloni*, free in theory, were in fact bound to the land they worked and could not move or marry out of their master's territories without his permission. There was little difference by the third century between the slave and the *colonus*.

Even the army, the 'military militia', as it was called to distinguish it from the 'official or administrative militia', was infected with the caste system. The legions, of old the instrument of aggression and victory, where valour and fortitude had been cultivated by real Romans, were latterly recruited exclusively from the dregs of the free population; conscription of rural recruits was made the responsibility of the wealthy senatorial class which, like the dwindling group of slaves, was excluded from military service. Service in the militia was no longer regarded as honourable: the legion, once 6,000 strong, was, under

Constantine, seldom a sixth of that, although by then many more legions were under arms than the twenty or thirty which had been enough under Trajan and Hadrian. Small wonder that only rough provincials, wild warriors from the perimeter of the Empire, provided the main body of the army. It had once been an attraction of a military career that it either conferred or led to Roman citizenship. As time went on that became less coveted as a reward and it is hardly surprising that barbarians alone in the fourth century regarded service in the army as worth while or proved themselves to be able commanders. As barbarians pressed in upon the shrinking rim of the Empire in the fourth and fifth centuries, Roman defence was usually successful in so far as it was conducted by troops only one stage less barbarous than their opponents.

This general relaxation of the Empire, increasing provincialism, an un-Roman army, were not matched by a lack of will at the centre. On the contrary, some remarkable emperors arose who were conscious of the *malaise* of the State. To their efforts, and notably to the efforts of Diocletian and Constantine, we must ascribe the success which in some measure attended those brutal arrangements we have touched on, the regimentation of every social activity. Everything that could be done by imperial edict was done, and harshness was often tempered by a charming paternalism: savage customs, like the exposure of sick slaves, were condemned; the rights of orphans were protected; a whole host of laws were concerned to shield the weak from the strong. It was, indeed, during the later centuries of the Empire, and particularly in the eastern Empire under Justinian, that Roman law acquired its final form, codified, civilized, resourceful: an elaborate legal structure which had so little real scope in the dreary days when it was being perfected (the very reiteration of imperial commands being a sufficient commentary on their ineffectiveness), but which, as we shall see, was to be revived to some purpose by a later age (below, p. 197).

In two important respects, however, the Roman world of the third and later centuries was composed of more enduring material: language and religion. Language, be it noted, and not literature, for the literary tradition of Rome, so vital in the late Republic and the Augustan period, was desperately ill-served by the handful of savants and the few academies, the pedestrian poets and rhetorical writers of the third and later centuries.[1] It was at this stage, indeed, that scholarship became a mere knowledge of grammar, literary ability consisted in the composition of *pastiches*, and the classical writers were read usually in epitomes. These features of Dark Age and early medieval literature were contributed by the late Empire: it was the latter-day Romans, in effect, who mislaid so much of Livy and made it possible for later generations to turn Virgil into a magician. Yet by the time that this loss of inspiration had attacked literature (and it was equally felt in science, philosophy, and the fine arts), the Latin language was as firmly entrenched in the provinces of the western Empire, as Greek in the eastern. Gaul, Spain, Italy of course, and Illyria had been Roman for so long that the language

---

[1] There are, of course, some notable exceptions, especially certain of the Christian Fathers, e.g. Jerome and Augustine.

of the conquered peoples were almost totally submerged by what (significantly enough) was called, not Latin, but *lingua Romana*, the 'romance language'. Even in the so-called classical period it seems likely that a wide gulf separated written literature from spoken or vulgar Latin; soon dialects developed which, after a further infusion of barbarian speech, were to crystallize later as French, Spanish, Italian and other Romance tongues. Britain and the Balkan and North African provinces had never been so thoroughly Romanized and were, in any case, subjected to larger and more damaging invasions later on. There Latin was almost entirely wiped out. But in the older area of Roman domination the Rhine and the Alps remain to this day an enduring linguistic boundary.

Christianity is the other immediate contribution of Rome. At first the religion of the followers of Christ was confined to a comparatively small number. It spread where there were Jews, and there were Jews in most of the big towns of the Mediterranean area. Thence it gradually attracted Gentile adherents. It was a time when the severity of the older Roman religion had for the most part been dissolved into scepticism among the cultivated and superstition among the rest. The transcendental religions of the East had considerable appeal. Isis and Mithras were the weightiest of the rivals for popular favour and, in general, Christianity was too intransigeant, too much an affair of abnegation and retreat, to make rapid headway. The early Christian instinctively rejected the World, accepted persecution as his lot, and—even when, like St. Augustine, imbued with the best that the Latin culture of the time could produce—tried to abandon the heritage of Hellenistic tradition in science, philosophy, and literature. In his *City of God* (426) St. Augustine drew a bold line through the totality of experience. On the one hand lay the earthly city, whose citizens aimed only at profits and peace here below: on the other hand the heavenly city, whose citizens lived on earth as pilgrims, 'as if they were in captivity'. This division was to have far-reaching consequences, but as a picture of the attitude of the majority of Christians in his own day, early in the fifth century, it was sadly out of focus. Almost a century before St. Augustine wrote his *City of God*, the Emperor Constantine had taken the first momentous steps towards the official recognition of Christianity by the 'earthly city', the Roman State which had hitherto been its enemy.

In 313 the Emperor in the 'Edict of Milan' granted religious liberty to 'Christians and all men' (*et Christianis et omnibus*). This, in fact, was a favour to Christians rather than to 'all men'; from being persecuted Christians were now to live 'without any anxiety or hurt', without being mulcted by rapacious officials, with full legal protection for themselves and their buildings. For some, Constantine's action seemed part of a divine intervention in human affairs; this was the view Christians took at the time, and it was accompanied by a tradition that Constantine had had a vision, had been dramatically converted to the new faith. For others, Constantine seems to have played a cynical role, the shrewd politician seeking to bolster the tottering Empire with a dynamic moral force. Others again have argued that he was neither devout nor sceptical, but profoundly superstitious, seeing his lucky star in the sky over Bethlehem; they would add that the relatively small number of Christians in the early fourth century were divided among themselves by bitter doctrinal disputes, and that they were most influential in the eastern half of the Empire where the reinforcement of imperial authority was least needed. But in a sense such speculations are beside the point. What is of supreme importance is that within a short space of time Constantine's successors persecuted non-Christians, turned Christianity into an official cult, absorbed the other-worldly Church into the wordly State.

The results were profoundly to affect both Church and State. The Emperor became, in a very real sense, head of the Church and regarded it as his duty to intervene even in the most complicated theological questions. It thus came about that the doctrine of Arius, which solved a Christian paradox by denying the divinity of Christ, was condemned by Constantine and the Council of Nicea in 325, despite the many adherents which its simplicity secured for it, especially among the barbarians; some later emperors, it is true, supported Arianism, but by that time the Nicene Creed had established itself, above all in the western Empire. The emperors who summoned councils, appointed patriarchs and bishops, were indeed almost priestly in their own persons. They had shed the divine attributes of their pagan predecessors only to don a quasi-apostolic garb and in art they were frequently depicted bearing the halo of sanctity. The effects on the ordinary believer were in the long run to be equally disturbing. The Christian now had behind him the resources of imperial authority and by the fifth century the new religion could claim the allegiance of a majority of Romans. Christianity and civilization were thus made coterminous; only the rustic, the *paganus*, was not a member of the Church. The bishops, already established in many towns, became the representatives, not merely of the emperor, but of Roman culture, a part which the average bishop was well equipped to play since he came usually from the upper classes. The faithful no longer assembled in furtive secrecy, but took possession of old temples and built new ones of their own. The rigorous practice of a holy life ceased to be possible for all Christians, and became more and more the job of a specialized priestly calling.

Bishops and priests, indeed, were themselves so intimately bound up with secular matters that, in the confused and troubled world of the fifth and sixth centuries, merely to be a priest seemed inadequate to those who longed for God. True, by every reasonable means the hierarchy of clergy which was gradually emerging under patriarchs and pope sought to differentiate the order of priesthood, and make it pure as well as efficient. Such aims led to the growing authority of certain bishops over other bishops in their vicinity, of bishops over the subordinate clergy in their dioceses, and an attempt was made to enforce celibacy on all ordained servants of God. Yet, to the devout, these measures were mere palliatives. A strain of Oriental mysticism was, after all, implicit in the Scriptures and soon many Christians separated themselves physically from the world, to live as isolated hermits or in small communities. It was for the direction of a community which had withdrawn from the world that St. Benedict of Nursia drew up in 529 his rule (*regula*). This brilliant organization of devotion, which is at the root of every later monastic development, was based on the authority of the abbot, Christ's vice-regent in each monastery, on the supreme virtue of obedience, and on the necessity of work, both manual and intellectual, as the main spur to an athletic faith. Clothed in a special uniform, living in a building dedicated to God, with every minute of the day allocated to prayer and labour, the monk took upon himself a way of life distinct not only from the corrupt lay society beyond the monastery wall, but from the priestly order which ministered directly to the laity, the *secular* clergy.

The Roman Empire had thus created a Church which was fundamentally Roman: Roman in its attitude to the theoretically omnipotent emperor, in its organization by cities, in its adoption of Latin as a vehicle of prayer and praise, in its practical identification with the limits of Roman power. Even the monastic movement, which was in a sense a reaction from the compromises involved in the adoption of Christianity as the official creed of the mass of Roman citizens, reveals an authoritarianism, a respect for law, an itch for system, which bears witness to the strength possessed by these characteristically Roman attitudes in the sixth century and later. We shall see further evidence for the vitality of certain Roman qualities and concepts in the next chapter.

CHAPTER II

THE MIGRATIONS AND SETTLEMENT OF THE BARBARIANS

Reasons for barbarian pressure on the Empire; the settlements; barbarians accept and emulate the Empire; Greek Church centred on Byzantine Emperor; Latin Church on Bishop of Rome; nature of barbarian kingdoms; the last invasions.

FROM the second century the northern borders of the Empire had to withstand increasing pressure from the German tribes beyond. From an even earlier date barbarians had penetrated into the Empire as slaves and as soldiers. This dilution of the Roman Empire was greatly accelerated during the fourth century and from 410 (when Rome was occupied by Alaric and his Visigoths) the area previously dominated by Rome was shaken by four centuries of invasion. The Germans and Slavs were followed in waves by remoter tribes, Huns, Tartars, Magyars; the Norsemen came down from Scandinavia; Moslem armies swept through Asia Minor and North Africa to attack the European mainland in both east and west. However strong the Empire might have been it could never have countered such massive blows, delivered with century-long persistence and from every quarter of the compass. Yet it would be a mistake to suppose that the invasions were prompted

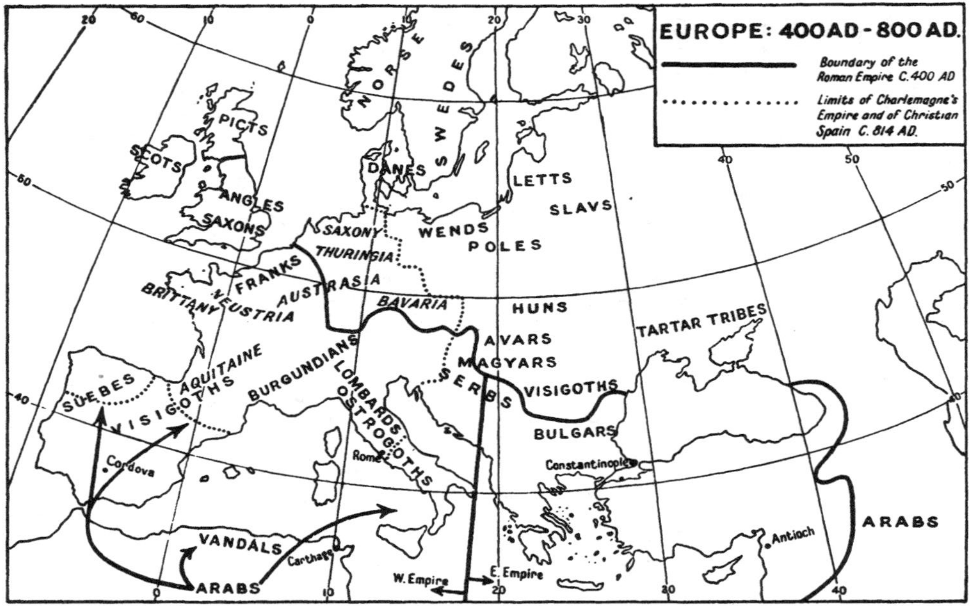

MAP I

EUROPE: 400 AD - 800 AD.

―― Boundary of the Roman Empire C.400 AD
······ Limits of Charlemagne's Empire and of Christian Spain C. 814 AD.

solely by a desire to seize on the wealth of the Mediterranean world at a time when it could not be well defended. That wealth, as we have seen, was almost non-existent. From the third century real power in the Roman world lay in the hands of a senatorial class living in its country villas, rich in possessions which could scarcely be stolen, hordes of armed retainers, self-sufficient estates, and immunity from taxation—rich in fact only by comparison with the wretched and dwindling populations of the dying towns, those 'corpses of cities', as they were called by St. Ambrose (d. 397). Indeed these magnates had often more in common with the tribal chieftains beyond the limits of the Empire than they had with the Emperor, desperately struggling with his barbarian generals and troops to stem the tide of invasion; and the emperors themselves, surrounded by outlandish companions and depending on success in battle for their hourly survival, were in a sense nearer to the war leaders of their opponents, the Alarics and Attilas, than to their predecessors from Septimius Severus to Constantine.

As the Empire contracted under barbarian assaults, moving eastwards towards the New Rome, Constantinople, the provinces of the Balkans, Greece, and Asia Minor stood out as infinitely more civilized than those in the West. By concentrating on the defence of the East the later emperors preserved, not a Latin culture certainly (for Latin was gradually dropped at Byzantium in favour of Greek), but a tradition in which Latin elements mingled with Greek. This, together with the tremendous building activities of Constantine and Justinian, made the capital city shine bright, not only in the dark days of the fourth to seventh centuries, but right through the medieval period and beyond. The policy of establishing the imperial headquarters in Constantinople was brilliantly justified, for this city, unlike Rome, had a genuine economic vitality. Sited at the junction of the two great inland seas, at the meeting-place of the trade routes going north into what was to be Russia, east into Asia, and south into Syria, Egypt, and Africa, Constantinople had a natural wealth which was able to sustain the Empire for more than a thousand years.

If we can scarcely account for the barbarian invasions by attributing them to the covetousness of primitive peoples for a higher civilization, how are we to explain them? No simple answer is possible. It seems likely that the German and Slav tribes dwelling in the area of modern Germany and Austria (Franks, Saxons, Alemanni, Sueves) had passed over to a semi-pastoral economy and, with their more sedentary way of life, probably experienced a rise of population which may have encouraged expansion. Farther east, in the area north of the Danube occupied by modern Romania, dwelt the Visigoths (the 'Wise Goths') and, farther east still, between the Dneiper and the Bug, lay the Ostrogoths (the 'Bright Goths'). These tribes, nomadic and savage, scarcely softened by the Arian Christianity which had reached them, as it had also reached some of the German tribes already mentioned, had even more redoubtable neighbours on the vast steppes crossed by the Don and Volga. These were the Huns, a migratory people habitually divided by feuds between clans, but capable of delivering devastating attacks when organized into a horde by a leader, fast-moving, irresistible and pitiless. Balked of an eastward expansion, it seems, by the resolute defence of successive Chinese emperors, and notably by the construction of the Great Wall (*c.* 214 B.C.), the Huns moved westwards with the centuries, and their steady but relentless surge was the main impulse to the drift of the more vulnerable tribes already mentioned.

The Roman emperors, as we have seen, attempted to defend their Empire by using the barbarians. The frontier was manned by tribes settled on land in return for military service, the legions were recruited from Germans and Goths, and more aggressive groups were admitted into the Empire as auxiliaries. Such soldiers were hardly reliable: Visigoths established south of the Danube by Valens in 376, defeated and slew him in a major battle near Adrianople in 378; Alaric, leader of the same Visigoths, had the imperial title of *magister militum* when he led his forces westwards towards Italy, and the leader of the 'Roman' armies facing him in Italy was Stilicho, a Vandal. When the 'Roman' towns were full of barbarian troops nominally in 'Roman' employment, when many of the agricultural workers were barbarians, when whole areas were set aside for theoretically 'allied' tribes, it is hard to speak of the Empire being defended, at any rate in the West. By dint of encouraging its formidable neighbours to press ever farther westwards the area round Constantinople was held, and the emperors in the East even staved off the attacks of the Sassanid rulers of Persia. But in the West the old provinces of Italy, Gaul, Spain, and Britain were submerged.

In large groups and small the barbarians moved into the Empire, usually avoiding strong-points and settling where resistance was light; ever moving farther on, Visigoths crossing Burgundian territory, Vandals moving past Franks and Sueves, the vast kaleidoscopic transformation was constantly stirred and rearranged. In 476 the last emperor at Rome was finally put aside by Odoacer who, like his successor Theodoric (493-526), was termed 'patrician' and regarded in some sense as a deputy of the eastern emperor. But while the Roman cities of Italy (especially Rome itself, Ravenna and Naples), continued to harbour sympathy for Constantinople, the emperor had no direct rule in the West. Britain had succumbed to Angles and Saxons. Northern Gaul was in the hands of Frankish tribes, while the Burgundians were in the Rhone valley and the Visigoths straddled the Pyrenees. In North Africa, formerly the main source of Italian food supplies, the Vandals had established themselves after a sojourn in Spain. Everywhere, but more especially in southern Gaul and Italy, there were pockets of Romans and Romanized barbarians, but these groups had lost the will to do more than defend themselves, and Odoacer's deposition of Romulus Augustulus in no sense deprived these western Romans of a leader. Roman leadership, such as it was, lay in the hands of the Church: the papacy was to be a more resilient opponent of barbarism than the Empire.

The year 476 thus seems to be less critical than used to be thought. Far from destroying the Empire, Odoacer considered himself to have united it again under the undivided authority of the emperor at Constantinople. Odoacer's respect for the forms of the past was shared by the other chieftains established in the West. It was their aim, as it was the aim of the emperors, to legitimize the situation by invoking the elastic nomenclature of older days. Even in its palmiest days Rome had not scrupled to tolerate subject princes. Was not Herod a king? The rulers of the newly established kingdoms sought approval at Constantinople; Odoacer was termed 'patrician'; Euric, the Visigothic master of Spain, was recognized by the Emperor Zeno; Burgundian princes were granted the title of *magister militum*; Clovis, king of the Franks, was in 508 given the title of proconsul. In a sense these titles were more than justified, for it was the Franks and Visigoths established in Gaul, under the leadership of a Roman provincial called Aetius, who had defeated the most terrible of all the Asiatic incursions, that of Attila and the Huns. At the battle of Chalons (probably near Troyes) in 451 Attila's horde was turned back; Attila's death two years later completed the discomfiture and led to the dispersal of the Huns. Even in the sixth century the scene in the West must have seemed to the emperor little different from what it had been for three centuries past. The kinglets angling for recognition at Constantinople, the pope regarding himself as an imperial representative, these were evidence of the prestige of the Empire and it needed only a little force to reassert the power of New Rome in the whole of the Mediterranean basin. To this task Justinian devoted himself. Between 533 and 563 his generals Belisarius and Narses were successful in destroying the power of the Vandals in North Africa, in reclaiming the eastern seaboard of Spain, and in dominating the Italian peninsula. Such a victory, however, needed large garrisons and numerous administrators if it was to be exploited, and these the Empire could not afford: it was at war with Persia continuously and Slav tribes were pressing into the Balkans. The north of Italy was engulfed from 568 by a fresh wave of barbarians, the Lombards (who made no pretence of acting in the name of the emperor), and the reconquest of Justinian melted away. Yet even in the tenth century the reigning Byzantine emperor could talk to an emissary of Otto I as though Rome, Italy, and the West was his for the taking: 'You are not Romans but Lombards', was the contemptuous remark which the Emperor Nicephorus threw at Liudprand bishop of Cremona in 968.

The continuity of the Empire in the West, which so sadly misled a tenth-century emperor, was nevertheless based on more solid grounds than a temporary desire to unite against the terror of the Huns, even if it was not sufficient to allow of a simple reoccupation as planned by Justinian. The barbarians and their chieftain kings took over what remained of Roman administration; they took over the Latin language; and they were Christians, although at first of the Arian sort.

The king tried to behave with the despotic authority of his Byzantine model, and the popular assembly, which of old had been the source of authority in German or Gothic tribal life, waned in importance. In Spain the Visigothic kings even made a pretence of legislation in the Roman style, and in Spain too the old administrative divisions of the original provinces were to some extent maintained. In Italy town life continued on a reduced scale under both Ostrogoths and Lombards. Everywhere, among Franks, Burgundians, Goths, Lombards, and Vandals an attempt was made to keep alive the financial basis of Roman administration, the treasury or fisc; and the evil reputation which the Vandals later acquired was in part due to the violence with which they exacted taxes in the lands they had conquered.

The willing adoption of Roman habits is revealed equally in the rapidity with which the invaders abandoned their own languages in favour of Latin. Within a few generations the Goths, the Franks, and other barbarians were linguistically assimilated, though they contributed many basic words to the Romance dialects of French, Spanish, and Italian. 'Peace' (*pax*) they learned to say in Latin: 'war' (*guerra*) they taught the Roman provincials to adopt; and so in many other instances the technical language of the warrior class remained Teutonic in origin, while the simple vocabulary of the home and the field were of Latin derivation. Only the clergy needed to cope with the cultures which fused at the same time as the languages; and they ensured that here, and especially in literature, Latin values not only survived but in many ways imposed themselves on the less developed and more impermanent art of the conquerors. As early as 622 in Visigothic Spain the tattered traditions of Roman science, philosophy, and literature were gathered together by Isidore of Seville in his *Etymologiae*, an encyclopaedic work of reference. Pitifully meagre, written in a Latin which betrayed at every turn the linguistic isolation of its author, this book, together with St. Augustine's *City of God* and Boethius's *Consolation of Philosophy* (523) and his translation of some Greek philosophers, was to furnish the next six centuries with the basis of its knowledge of the ancient world.

When Isidore of Seville was writing, Visigothic Spain had ceased to be Arian for some thirty years. In Gaul and in Italy the victory of the Nicene Creed or rather of its Roman defenders was accomplished earlier. The Roman bishops were everywhere at their posts when the invaders settled, surrounded by a 'familia' of clergy, at once a school for priests and an administrative headquarters for the bishop's 'parish' or diocese. The Roman episcopate was better educated, came of a better class, was more conscious of a centralizing mission, than the isolated, ignorant, and humble Arian presbyters. Intermarriage between conqueror and conquered also bridged the religious gap while the political need to consolidate subjugated lands gave kings an obvious inducement to conform to a faith which in any case made them better able to sustain a royal part. As a result Arianism rapidly collapsed as a rival to Catholicism. Shortly after 500 the pagan Clovis, King of the Franks, was baptized into the Roman religion of his wife, and so were 3,000 of his warriors. The new Christian proved a bitter enemy of his Arian neighbours to the south, and in a short time the victory of the Franks ensured a Catholic instead of an Arian Gaul. In Italy the Ostrogoths were also Arians, although they were extremely tolerant of their Roman subjects, especially under the intelligent rule of Theodoric. It was partly as a crusade against heretics that Justinian attempted the reconquest of the West, and his destruction of Ostrogothic power was a victory for the orthodox faith. The Lombards, who then submerged northern Italy, undid this for a while, but they were a more backward people than the Goths and, though at first bitterly hostile to the

Roman Church, they had completely abandoned their lightly-held Arianism by the end of the seventh century.

Another variant form of Christianity was also eliminated at about the same time. Christianity had early penetrated Ireland from Britain, and when Britain was conquered by the pagan Angles and Saxons, Irish Christians, cut off from the mainland, developed an exotic Church organization, marked, from St. Patrick onwards, by a strong evangelical spirit. In the sixth century Irish missionaries turned eastwards, St. Columba to Scotland, Columban and his followers to Gaul, Italy, and Germany: Iona in the western islands of Scotland, Luxeuil in France, Bobbio in Italy, St. Gall in Switzerland were some of the more famous of the monastic establishments created by this movement. The continental outposts of Celtic Christianity were soon absorbed into the main stream of Roman orthodoxy, and, starting in 596, St. Augustine of Canterbury and his successors gradually succeeded in bringing England into line. The mingling of the two traditions in Northumbria was fruitful; the generation which followed the elimination of Celtic heterodoxy, at the Synod of Whitby in 663, produced the last great figure in classical Latin literature, the Jarrow monk Bede, whom later ages surnamed the Venerable.

The religious uniformity of the West was accomplished by 700, although in many areas Christianity was as yet only a thin veneer spread over a fundamental paganism. For the next 500 years no heresy worth the name was to develop in this area, in striking contrast with the East, where, besides Arianism, other great controversies over the nature of Christ were to rend the Church, the Nestorians and Monophysites breaking away to found schismatic Churches of their own. But in the East the emperors continued to regard the Church as a department of State; 'heretics' were all too frequently political opponents of the ruling emperor; and the external enemies of Byzantium were ready to foment religious disunity, Persian kings, for instance, allowing the Nestorians to settle in their lands. Nothing so well illustrates imperial authoritarianism as the decision of Leo III in 726 to abolish the worship of holy images (eikons), a practice deeply rooted in both East and West, and one which had been positively encouraged in the past as a way of simplifying religion for recently converted pagans. The riots and counter-revolutions provoked by the iconoclastic dispute raged for more than a century, but the long-term results were of even greater importance. In art the compromise finally adopted in the East was responsible for the stylized and remote approach of Byzantine artists to the depiction of sacred subjects, a tradition which was to have its most distant and moving exponent in El Greco, the Greek, in the sixteenth century. In everyday religion, the emotional differences between East and West were intensified; the cult in the East became gradually less intimately associated with the congregation; the sacrament in the Greek rite (celebrated behind the iconostasis, the screen or wall separating the sanctuary from the body of the church), was not, like the Roman Mass, a dramatic conjunction of priest and people.

If the emperors in the East were partly responsible for the religious turmoil which made every barber in Constantinople a theologian, the architect of uniformity in the less sophisticated West was the papacy. Everything conspired to this end. Of the senior churches, founded by or associated with the apostles, Rome was the only one in the West, its chief rival, Carthage, having been eliminated by the Vandals: the other patriarchates, Antioch, Jerusalem, and Constantinople,[1] besides being frequently at loggerheads through schism and heresy, had a more restricted obedience. By the end of the third century the 'Pope' (*papa*, father) was known by that name, and in 343 the Council of Sardica authorized appeals to the bishop of Rome. It was inevitable that the provincial clergy should look to Rome, that the bishop of the City should be pre-eminent in the Empire. When the emperors withdrew to the East, when the provincial administration crumbled or was clumsily manipulated by barbarian chiefs, the Roman Church remained more or less intact, while the prestige of the bishop of Rome, still imperially appointed or confirmed, grew immeasurably. Despite their venality and immorality, their domination by Gothic or Lombard magnates, their humiliation by Justinian and his generals, the popes were elevated by the pressure of the provincial clergy, eager to have an authority which would do something to protect them against Arian princelings, which still adhered in principle to the integrity of Roman law, and which could uphold their traditions against, or interpret their policy towards, the emperor at Constantinople. Moreover, in the troubled state of Italy the pope's power as a magistrate in Rome and its vicinity was large and ill-defined; his estates, scattered over the

[1] Constantinople was not an apostolic patriarchate like the others, but was declared one by the Council of Chalcedon (451).

whole peninsula, were rich and relatively well-managed; his relationships with Goth and Lombard had no need to be intransigeant, like those of the official imperial representatives, the exarchs at Ravenna, but could admit of compromise and conciliation. Such a politic approach is revealed in the doctrine outlined by the fifth-century pope, Gelasius I: 'Thus there are two powers', he wrote to the Emperor Anastasius I, 'by which this world is chiefly ruled—the pontifical and the regal.'[1] This was a sound basis for creating an understanding between the papacy and the new kingdoms of the West, however unpalatable it was at the time to the autocrat at Byzantium, however illogical it was to be proved by the later history of the popes.

Not all the popes of the fifth, sixth, and seventh centuries were content to allow time and chance to determine their own fate and the fate of their religion. In particular the tendencies we have observed were deliberately encouraged by Gregory I, the Great. He, more than any other individual, was responsible for ending Arianism in Spain and Italy, and for bringing the Celtic Church into the Roman communion. Himself both a monk and an ex-prefect of the City, he realized the worth of monasticism as a spiritual arm of papal government, and of the temporal power of the bishop of Rome as a protection against lay intimidation. Rigidly insisting on the oecumenical character of papal authority as against the claim of the patriarch of Constantinople, Gregory

[1] 'As between these,' he goes on, 'the priestly power is of greater weight (*gravius est pondus sacerdotum*), for priests are answerable to God for Kings.' But in Gelasius's doctrine it was the equality of the two 'powers' that later ages chose to remember.

did his best to exalt episcopal responsibility not only by practice but also by precept, his treatise on a bishop's duties, the *Cura Pastoralis*, becoming the most widely known of his books. Yet it was in this pontificate, with the papacy firmly on the road to its later grandeur, that, in the superscription in papal letters, the pope's name was first qualified by the phrase *servus servorum Dei*, 'servant of the servants of God'.

The continuity and the authority of the Church of Rome stood out in marked contrast against not only the turbulent heresies and imperial control of the Church in the East, but also against the short-lived kingdoms which rose and fell in the West. With the detailed history of the Visigoths, Sueves, Vandals, Ostrogoths, and Lombards we cannot here concern ourselves. But the elements of the story may be summarised with depressing brevity. Again and again the kings of these barbarian States asserted their authority only to fail to hand it on undivided. Partly this was because their aim at a Byzantine type of monarchy was over-ambitious, given the lack of financial resources in the West; partly it was because Germanic tradition in private law sanctioned the division of a father's lands among his sons, and this practice was adopted by kings so that the sanctity of monarchy as well as the estates of the king were shared by several heirs and the unified control of large areas was at the mercy of accidents of descent; partly it was because the intrigues of neighbouring princes and of the Emperor himself, together with occasional raids by Huns or Avars, perpetuated and aggravated the disequilibrium. But behind these causes of royal instability lay a trouble more fundamental still: the reality of power resided no longer in the possession of a title to monarchy, but in the control of land. The breadth of a man's estates was the measure of his political influence. The Crown itself was compelled to buy support by alienating its territories to magnates. Dukes and counts (*duces, comites*) were rewarded not with cash but with fields and forests. The very exercise of royal power denuded a monarch of his power to command. Only a successful war could temporarily fill royal coffers and re-endow the king with fresh territory. Every spring an efficient king tried to lead his warriors on aggressive expeditions. With peace came poverty.

The truth of these general remarks may be illustrated from the history of the Franks, where two more than usually ambitious and fortunate dynasties emerged for a short space. The Franks were established in the area of the rivers Seine, Meuse, and Rhine, and by the end of the fifth century, though those inhabiting the Rhine area were united under one king, those to the south-west of this were ruled by several chieftains. It was one of these, Clovis the Merovingian,[1] King of Tournai, who seized every chance offered to him of enlarging his dominions. So successful was he that he dominated the neighbouring Franks, penetrated southwards beyond the Loire, and by 507 had destroyed the power of the Alemanni, a German tribe in the upper Rhine area. His conquests were followed by the settlement of his Frankish followers, but usually on vacant land, or on land belonging to the Empire, so that the inhabitants of the occupied area were not seriously threatened by

[1] The dynasty was termed 'Merovingian' from Merovée, a reputed ancestor of Clovis.

his advance. Moreover, though himself at first a pagan, Clovis was considerate of the Catholic clergy, and his conversion, as we have already seen, facilitated the subjugation of the Arian Burgundians and the acquisition of Aquitaine from the Visigoths. Once a Roman Christian, Clovis then became a Roman proconsul and, when he died in 511, he was the legitimate ruler of an area roughly comparable to modern France which, in a sense, he had created and to which his people gave their name. Yet on Clovis's death the kingdom was divided among his four sons and for a century 'Francia' or Frankland was disturbed by chaotic dynastic feuds, marked by savage brutality and a total absence of royal authority. True, the royal descent was still honoured; the sons of Clovis were followed by their grandsons; and ultimately in 613 it was a great-grandson of Clovis who reigned once more over a theoretically reunited country. This was Chlotar II, who was followed by his son Dagobert, in whom some of Clovis's vigour was renewed.

There were, however, by now three distinct areas in the kingdom, partly as a result of earlier settlement, partly as a result of the upheavals following Clovis's death; Neustria (or West Francia), north of the Loire almost to the Meuse, but excluding Brittany, which had been seized and colonized by Britons, fleeing from the country which was to be known as England; Austrasia (East Francia), the valleys of the Meuse and lower Rhine; and Burgundy, the centre and south-east of present-day France. In each of these areas Chlotar II and Dagobert were compelled to appoint 'Mayors of the palace', local grandees; when the monarchy again split up under

Merovingian princes after Dagobert, such power as pertained to the Crown was wielded by the mayor of the palace in each of these parts of Francia, the nominal ruler being regarded, in a classical phrase, as a *roi fainéant*. Each great magnate sought his own interest, and for a time it seemed as though Francia might entirely disintegrate; Aquitaine, for instance, under a series of able dukes, succeeded in separating itself from the body of the kingdom, and Frankish control of German tribes in Saxony and Thuringia was lost. Yet, if the throne was weak, there was always a chance for the power behind the throne, the mayor of the palace, to persuade his fellow-magnates towards aggressions which might prove mutually rewarding. The signal success enjoyed by Ebroin, mayor of the palace of Neustria, was a portent: by 679 he had destroyed all resistance to his authority in Burgundy and Austrasia.

Ebroin was assassinated in 681, however, and within ten years the whole of Francia recognized another master, Pepin of Herstal, mayor of the palace of Austrasia. His bastard, Charles Martel (the Hammer), who gave his name to the Carolingian dynasty, maintained his father's ascendancy and the Franks, under the leadership of these two princes, penetrated farther than ever before into Germany. But on Charles Martel's death in 741 the lands he had ruled were divided between his two sons, and only the abdication of one left the other, Pepin the Short, as ruler of a single realm. Pepin deposed the titular Merovingian king and ruled in his own name, one result of a momentous alliance with the papacy which was threatened at the time by Lombard attacks and deprived of effective help from the emperor at Constantinople. King Pepin's territories were divided on his death in 768, yet unity was again preserved by the death of one of the heirs.

The new king, Charles, was an even more successful ruler than his predecessors. Charlemagne (Carolus Magnus) grasped his opportunities firmly; he destroyed the Lombards and enriched himself and the papacy with Italy north of Rome; he stormed south beyond the Pyrenees, north to convert the Saxons to Christianity and subjection to the Franks, east to absorb the already Christian Bavaria, farther east still to shatter the Avars and create a marcher dependency in Carinthia. Master of the West, master of the Church and the pope, Charles was the reincarnation of the masterful emperors of the early Roman Empire. The clerks in his court were conscious enough of the comparison. Had not his father been made a patrician by Byzantium? Was it not fitting that the very highest legitimacy should attach to the Frankish master of so many of the old provinces? A grateful pope on Christmas Day, 800, crowned Charlemagne emperor in St. Peter's, Rome. This action, like Charles's ambitious attempts to govern his vast dominions, was to have important consequences later. For the moment it is sufficient to stress one point: the Carolingian Empire was ephemeral. It so happened that Charlemagne had only one heir, Lewis the Pious, when he died in 814, but he had earlier planned a partition of his Empire between Lewis and two other sons who did not survive; and when Lewis died in 840 the division was actually accomplished, the Empire disintegrating in the civil wars which followed.

A fundamental conservatism was in part

responsible for the brief domination of the Merovingian kings and the rulers of the other barbarian kingdoms, just as it was with the more imposing Carolingian edifice. Doubtless any monarchy was doomed to failure which tried to transcend the only relationship which society could tolerate at the time, the relationship based on control over land. But the kings of the Franks, like the kings of Italy and Spain, had not only to face the internal threat of powerful magnates, but even more formidable external enemies. The Visigoths, Ostrogoths, Franks and the rest had only begun to settle down and to organize themselves when, in succession, from south, north, and east, fresh waves of invaders surged forwards, Moslems, Northmen, Magyars.

In 622 the prophet Mohammed moved from the wealthy commercial city of Mecca in southern Arabia, which had rejected his divine message, to Medina. This is the Hegira, or Emigration, with which the Moslem begins his era. Mohammed found his new home more sympathetic to the puritanical monotheism he was preaching, and, having mastered Medina, he turned to the conversion of the whole of Arabia. Though he resorted to force and played skilfully on the rivalries of the Bedouin tribes, his sense of mission was his chief resource, while the coherence of the system he advocated was welcome to the tribesmen in their relationship with the more sophisticated neighbouring peoples—Persians and Greeks, Christians and Jews. By the time Mohammed died in 632, he was master of vast hordes of Arab soldiers, and hostility to the peoples of the north characterized both the Prophet and the Faithful. Once the feebleness of the eastern Empire was apparent, and it was in 634 that the Byzantines were first defeated by the Moslems in Palestine, the caliphs, who suceeded Mohammed as rulers of Islam, sent tribe after tribe to scour the southern littoral of the Mediterranean, and to annex provinces and kingdoms to the true religion.

The detailed story of conquest cannot be repeated here, and it would only obscure the lightning rapidity of Moslem advance. Within a century of Mohammed's death the eastern Empire was battling for its life at the very gates of Constantinople, North Africa had been overrun and so had Spain, while the Persian Empire had been destroyed and Islam was already turning East. Against the disciplined Arab armies there was little that Visigothic Spain could do, and it was only the victory of Charles Martel at 'Tours' in 732 which prevented Francia from being likewise engulfed. At about the same time (717) Constantinople successfully resisted siege. These 'victories' were scarcely responsible for saving Christendom: the difficulty eastern emperors had in retaining, let alone extending their restricted control of Asia Minor, the limited success of Charlemagne in his attack on Moorish Spain, show how firm was the grip of Islam on the conquered lands; the occupation of Crete in 826, and the prolonged attempts to dominate Sicily and even southern Italy show how thoroughly the Arabs had mastered the sea. What saved Christendom were the schisms in Islam itself, which caused the flood of aggression to dry up. Finally emerging with three distinct political centres—Baghdad, Cairo, and Cordova, the Moslem world was no longer a danger as far as military force was concerned, though it continued to threaten Christianity in subtler ways which we will have later to consider (below, p. 212). While individual Moslem soldiers were often brutal and rapacious, Islam had all the strength of utter confidence in its civilizing mission and proved remarkably tolerant of diversity in its subject peoples.

The Northmen, who descended on the undefended Atlantic seaboard of Christendom at the end of the eighth century and whose attacks continued for a century, were infinitely more savage than the Arabs. The Teutonic peoples dwelling in Scandinavia had been isolated by the migrations of the fourth and fifth centuries. Their barren fjords familiarized them with the sea: their mountainous land offered no outlet for the tumultuous younger sons of a warrior class. Pirates with an instinct for a bargain which made them incline to commerce as well, they sailed solely for booty and were sustained by no religious fervour such as Islam gave its adherents. Over the Atlantic they reached Iceland and America, the Vinland of the Sagas: they crossed the Baltic and penetrated down the river routes to the Black Sea and Constantinople, setting up trading stations at Kiev and Novgorod (from which Russia was later to develop), and being hired as mercenaries by the Emperor. In Ireland, Scotland, and England, they came to ravage, later wintered in their victims' lands, and finally established permanent settlement. The same is true of the rivers and estuaries of Germany and Francia. But by about 900 the impetus of attack slackened and reinforcements ceased to reach the invaders who had established themselves. Ireland, northern Scotland, northern England (the Danelaw), and the area of Francia known as Normandy were the areas most closely affected by Viking colonization. Yet these terrible enemies of Christendom were soon devout Christians, and Christianity was travelling back to Scandinavia itself. The Northmen also absorbed the culture of the peoples they had ravaged, soon speaking their language and adopting the law and the social conventions which surrounded them. They were, after all, Germans, like the Angles and Franks.

The Magyars, on the contrary, were nomadic horsemen from the steppes of Asia, linguistically related to Finns and Turks. Towards the end of the ninth century they moved into modern Hungary and thence their raiding parties struck westwards into Germany, penetrating to the Rhine delta and the North Sea. Lombardy was terrorized in 899; Provence even was stricken in 924. Here again a century saw the violence of the assault weaken: the Magyars found their forays produced little permanent prosperity and they were often decimated by disease. It was not, however, until they were decisively beaten by Otto I in 955 at the battle of Lechfeld that they completely ceased their attacks, becoming Christians some fifty years later.

It is quite impossible to exaggerate the misery and insecurity produced by the Moslem, Viking, and Magyar attacks. The small and scattered communities of England, Francia, and Spain had no strong kings to organize defence: they lacked navies to protect them from Moslem and Norse sea power; the Magyars were only deterred by the walled cities of Italy, for elsewhere castles were usually wooden and other settlements even less protected. The magnates, with their retainers and some defensible site, could hope to avoid attack, or could bargain with the marauders to secure at any rate a partial immunity. But the population as a whole had only two alternatives: to stay and accept the terms of the raiders—in exactions of slaves or such mobile wealth as was available; or to evacuate threatened areas and seek safety in flight. This last was the plan adopted by the monks who had been established on the island of Noirmoutier off the mouth of the Loire in the seventh century. From this place they began moving each spring after 819 to Dées on the mainland. But in 836 they had permanently to abandon their island home, and the bones of their patron saint, St. Philibert, were carried a hundred miles away up the Loire valley in 858. Thence in 862 the monks moved on, southwards into Poitou; ten years later they moved 140 miles onwards to a site near Moulins; finally, in 875, at Tournus, near Macon, in Burgundy, they found a fortified *burg* and comparative security. In not much more than half a century the community had covered over 400 miles. This needed devotion, organization, and resources, which the poor and the isolated could scarcely command.

It was in this welter of violence and uncertainty that the last remnants of the older society collapsed. The last Carolingian 'emperor', Charles the Fat, was deposed in 887. Thenceforward monarchy depended, not on memories of Rome, but on the possession of military power based on land. The notion of the Empire was still to haunt men's imaginations, as we shall see. Yet later revivals, *renovationes*, renaissances were self-conscious and deliberate, totally different from the direct and involuntary inheritance of Roman language, institutions, and ideas which we have witnessed during the barbarian settlements.

Part II Manor, Feof, and Church

CHAPTER III

THE STRUCTURE OF SOCIETY

Geography and population of the European area c. A.D. 800; patterns of agrarian activity; the feudal relationship; knights, peasants, and changes on the manor; the clergy identified with feudal society, despite monastic reforms; literature, learning, universities; the 'Great Chain of Being'.

THE face of what we now call Europe was much wilder in 800 than it is today. Prehistoric man, with limited technical skills, had usually taken the easiest land to work. Over the centuries wide areas were, indeed, cleared by man and beast and at the height of its prosperity even remote provinces of the Roman Empire had extensive tracts of cultivated land. But in the later Empire there was regression, not least in the regions where the Romans and their subjects had practised intensive farming, and this was aggravated during the barbarian invasions. 'Natural' forest, heath, and marsh increased their hold even in Italy and Gaul. Farther north man had in any case done less to determine his geographical environment. The rim of inhospitable mountain which lies to the north of the Mediterranean was a formidable barrier and across the old Roman frontier, beyond the Rhine and the Danube, sprawled the vast Hercynian forest, the wooded hills of central Germany stretching from the Rhine to the Carpathians. The forests and the fenlands had, of course, their human denizens, the hunters, charcoal-burners, fishermen, but they were fewer in number than even the small groups of agriculturalists and shepherds settled in more favoured places.

We can only guess the size of the population of Europe for periods before regular censuses began (about 1800), and for periods before 1300 we must depend less on the figures of taxation assessments, parish registers and so forth, which gave us some concrete information from the fourteenth century onwards (below, p. 173), than on indirect demographic evidence: inventories of ecclesiastical domains ('polyptiques'), the sizes of peasant holdings from time to time, the changing areas encircled by the walls of towns, the extension of the land under cultivation or its contraction. The study of such intractable material does not enable us to say much more than that the population of Europe in the eighth and ninth centuries was very much smaller than it is nowadays. The proportion varied from country to country—England having perhaps only a fortieth of its present population, France a sixth—and from place to place within a country, the Île de France being more densely populated, for instance, than Brittany or Burgundy. That these small numbers were relatively more concentrated than they were to be later should not obscure their isolation. Such population as there was lived almost entirely in rural situations: towns were tiny at first, and for long even large towns had so many gardens and fields inside and immediately outside their walls that they resembled modern villages.

The size of the population was controlled by the vast and erratic forces of climate, pestilence, and war. The subsistence-economy practised in small hamlets made famine a recurrent reality, though the absence of long-distance trade in foodstuffs localized scarcity and did something to limit the spread of infectious disease. War was an affliction which was much more terrible if, in the long run, less inevitable. The predatory Romans had harried their conquests; when their control broke down the chieftains of the barbarians combined with the surviving landlords to ravage and dominate; finally the peasant faced the influx of Arabs, Danes, and Magyars. Apart from certain favoured areas in the Italian peninsula and in the eastern Mediterranean, the peasants of Europe had little rest in the first nine centuries of our era.

Given a period of relative peace the vitality of the peasant soon showed itself. The invasions were halted in the ninth and tenth centuries and, as stronger lordship everywhere guaranteed more stable political conditions, the population of Christendom began to rise; this inference seems inescapable from a study of what has been called 'the prehistoric period of demography'. How quickly the rise took place it is hard to say, but it was uninterrupted in most areas until the thirteenth century. This was due in the main to a relative prosperity which enabled more mouths to be fed: the 'expectation of life' was doubtless pitifully low by present standards, but the birth-rate was consistently high.

The increase in population was accommodated by an attack on the 'waste' and on the forest. Both had been useful in the past and had an economic role still to play. Grazing for swine, the hunting and snaring of wild beasts, big and small, firewood and timber for building, all came from land still in its natural state. But with land the only form of wealth and with the pressure of numbers resulting from more peaceful conditions, the relative importance of arable and meadow land on the one hand, and of waste on the other, changed. All groups took part in this vigorous 'internal colonization' of Christendom: the peasants who struck out into the forests to clear by hatchet and by fire, creating new villages and enlarging old ones; the lords, eager to increase their lands and their men; the Church, no less anxious for wealth and contributing to the process even in the very act of renunciation (for the Cistercians sought the wildest places for their monasteries and frequently turned them into fruitful farms). Nor were the even more ambitious tasks of draining marshes and reclaiming land from the sea avoided.

The peasants' activity, though it varied in detail from village to village, may be summarized without undue distortion. The pattern of agriculture was set by the geographical environment. Except where special conditions led to the cultivation of specialized crops (like olives, lemons, and silk in parts of the Mediterranean area, hemp and flax in the north), the farm was designed primarily to produce grain from arable land, while its meadows supported stock in summer and provided some precious hay to feed in winter the animals which were not slaughtered in the autumn. Apart from the cultivation of a small patch round his dwelling, the peasant farmed portions of the arable in the 'open' fields of the settlement. Of these there were either two or three, depending on the rotation of fallow and cultivation: in the 'two field system' each field lay fallow every other year; in the 'three field system', each field lay fallow every third year. These two or three great fields were not permanently enclosed and when under cultivation they were divided into strips, several of which were worked by each peasant family; among the peasants' strips were scattered those belonging to the lord of the estate, on which the peasants were required to work (below, p. 56). The settlement also normally included a meadow where cattle were grazed; the cattle were also turned on to the fallow field. Finally the adjacent forest and waste gave rough pasturage and feeding for pigs, firewood, timber, honey. The stream, besides watering the meadows, provided fish and motive power for the mills, which become common from the sixth century.

The type of cultivation we have described was practised in the richer lands of western Europe, in the lowland valleys of France, England, and western Germany. In upland centres, from Scotland to the Pyrenees, a different system is found. Known in Scotland as run-rig, this involved the temporary clearing of moorland and the farming of the land just cleared for a few years until its productivity was exhausted, when it was allowed to go to waste again and fresh fields were formed. The mountainous areas of Mediterranean Europe provided a third pattern of rural economy: in Spain, Italy, southern France, and the Balkans, the shepherd moved his flocks up the hills in the spring and down again at the end of summer (transhumance).

During the period we are concerned with, there was very little production designed for distant markets.

In the basic necessities of life each community was more or less self-sufficient. Each village settlement or group of settlements thus practised what is termed a 'subsistence-economy', depending on its own resources for food and the raw materials for housing and clothing. This is evident not only from the absence of specialized farming, but from the use of commodities for exchange; payments to the lord, for instance, were as often made in kind (eggs, chickens, grain), as in money. One must, however, not think of such a dependence on local production as barter. Money was always used in valuation, and cash was frequently employed even by the poorest. But minting was erratic, and (like the small markets and fairs) was local. There was 'monetary famine rather than a natural economy'. Of course some essential commodities were not obtainable in the vicinity. For example, the Swiss from an early date had to export dairy produce in exchange for grain. Salt had often to be brought from a distance, and so had wine. But it is significant that the production of both was then much more widely diffused: the vine was cultivated in lands as unpropitious as England and Poland.

The peasants who lived in the small and often isolated communities which slowly multiplied during the four centuries after 900 did not work only to keep themselves alive. Most of them had a master, or lord, though such 'seignorial' control was pretty tenuous in upland and mountain areas. Seignorial jurisdiction, lordship of land, was no new phenomenon. The possession of extensive legal and administrative rights over land and the peasantry on it was, at any rate in the richer areas, of very ancient date, and was destined to be characteristic of many parts of Europe until almost our own day. What lends a unique quality to the period we are now discussing is the way in which control over land was erected into a scheme of relationship not only between the master and his peasants, but between the masters themselves. This territorial organization of government was termed 'feudalism' by later ages, from the 'feof' or (in Latin) *feodum*, a name applied to the land held by one lord of another. How did the whole of society come to recognize feof-holding as the basis of political and legal, as well as of economic power? What were the main features of the feudal relationship?

In a sense one may attribute feudal institutions quite simply to a situation where land alone gave its possessors wealth, and where wealth was displayed by the ability to fight both for land already held and to obtain more land. Yet such an explanation would not define the phenomenon we are faced with. It would cover, for example, the looser tribal, clan, or village chieftainship which persisted throughout our period on the fringes of Christendom—in Ireland, western Scotland, northern Germany, Scandinavia, and which may still be found in some backward parts of the world today. Nor would so generalized a statement account for the geographical diffusion of feudalism. Found earliest in northern France and in Burgundy, feudal arrangements were always most highly developed there. From this centre the feudal principle radiated out over adjacent lands, becoming less coherent and stable the farther it travelled from its source. Eastwards it penetrated into Germany, but there its hold was erratic and its time-table of development retarded; to the south it entered Spain and Italy; to the west the Normans brought it to England, whence it penetrated into the lowlands of Scotland and into Ireland. Adventurers even planted it farther afield, in the Syrian lands conquered by the Crusaders. But it was never properly at home in eastern Europe or in the Byzantine Empire (see below, p. 125); as found even in Italy, Spain, and England it presents odd features which were never characteristic of the lands between Rhine and Loire which saw it first develop. This area had been the western frontier of Rome; it was the heart of the Merovingian and Carolingian kingdoms. Feudalism was historically due to the problems which faced the warriors who found themselves here in the early centuries of the Christian era.

A warrior class was to be found both in the Roman Empire itself and among the German tribes who penetrated it in the third and later centuries. The 'Roman' grandee, living in patriarchal and somewhat primitive style in the 'villa' at the heart of a great estate, had to look after himself in the later empire, if need be by force. Hence he tended often to enrol private soldiers, while many less powerful men were willing to enter into a client's relationship with him in return for protection. Among the German tribes the warriors grouped themselves round a war leader and gave their obedience to him in return for a share in booty. As the first invasions died down about 700 we find a word of Celtic origin being employed to cover the relationship of a free warrior to his master: he is a *vassus*, a 'vassal'. Soon something like a formal act was necessary to become a vassal, for one *commended oneself* into a magnate's entourage, where, in return for military service, one was given 'victuals and vestment'. The vernacular word in the language of the Franks was *maimbour*, which derives from *munt* = mouth, and *beran* = protection, a vivid illustration of a bread and butter relationship. One way the magnate could provide *maimbour*, victuals and vestment, protection, to the free dependent who would fight for him, was to give him a portion of land. Such land was, of course, not given him to work as a peasant, but to provide him with the necessities of life so that he could be his master's soldier; it was therefore a gracious act and was termed a 'benefice', a *beneficium*. In this age of little money and crude agricultural methods the master would naturally find it easier to provide for free retainers on his lands rather than in his immediate retinue. Moreover, scattered about his estates they acted as his deputies and formed a resident police force against internal and external enemies. The vassal enjoying his benefice, which constituted his protection and his upkeep, was by the eighth century a familiar feature of society in the north of France.

During Carolingian times, in the eighth and ninth centuries, conditions changed: the Frankish monarchy, which, as we have seen, aped Roman government, developed precociously; yet insecurity deepened with the raids of Moslems in the south, Norsemen in the north and west, and Magyars in the east. Even great magnates now found it useful to 'commend' themselves to greater potentates and above all to the king, whose powers in time of war had increased during the period of settlement. Equally the king sought to govern by conferring on his officers their duties *as benefices*. He called them by the late Roman titles *comites* (counts) and *duces* (dukes), but they and he regarded the office as similar to the benefice of land, naturally enough as the bulk of such offices were in fact territorial: the king nominated a magnate as count of Flanders or duke of Burgundy. When even the mightiest in the land were vassals, the status of all vassals was greatly elevated, while the wide diffusion of the free warrior-vassal was shown by the way in which the word 'man' was often used by itself to mean a member of the knightly or soldier class. 'Knight' or *chevalier* meant a mounted soldier for, largely under the influence of the mounted Slav and Magyar marauders, heavy cavalry became the main element in military power; and to be someone's 'man' meant almost automatically being his knight, as a vassal holding a benefice from him in return for services, and especially knight-service. Moreover the relationship of subjection between members of the free, knightly class was steadying into forms which were to last for centuries. The vassal placed his hands together and knelt before his future master. The master (or *senior*, *seigneur*, lord) put his hands round the vassal's hands. The vassal then stood up and, putting his hand on the Bible or a holy relic, swore his fealty for his lifetime and for his lord's lifetime. This process of becoming a lord's 'man' was termed homage (Fr. *homme* = a man). The benefice was then handed over in a further ceremony; some soil or a stick was given by the lord to his vassal; if he was being beneficed with a governmental appointment, such as a duchy, he was usually given a flag.

By the eleventh century the lord or *dominus* (in German *Herr*) and his vassal had identified the

THE STRUCTURE OF SOCIETY 49

military relationship and the benefice which was originally one of several distinct forms of sustenance. The benefice was given in return for services, services were rendered in return for a benefice. This mutual arrangement could be broken if either party failed in his duty. Fealty could be withdrawn by a formal act of *defiance* (literally = withdrawal of fealty) and, unless lord or man was prepared to accept this act, a state of hostility automatically ensued. The obligations of the parties to this verbal contract (it was only written down at first in legal form in the case of a few mighty princes) varied from place to place even in the Frankish and Burgundian homeland of feudalism. But usually the lord could expect his man to give him fealty, aid (*auxilium*) of a military kind and also of a money kind on certain specified crises (the lord's ransom if captured, the knighting of his eldest son, the dowry of his eldest daughter), and counsel or advice (when the knight attended his lord's court). The military service varied in relation to the size of the benefice. A vassal holding a large estate or group of estates owed his lord in war the service of himself and a correspondingly large number of knights. He in turn obtained the requisite number of knights by investing with smaller benefices the number of soldiers he required. (In practice he often invested *more* knights than he was actually called upon to produce.) On the other hand, the vassal could equally expect his lord's fealty, his protection (both military and in any courts of law where the knight might be prosecuted) and his material support, the benefice. It was also in the late tenth and eleventh centuries that the word 'benefice' was gradually replaced by the word 'feof' (a word of German origin, originally signifying cattle or movable wealth); the changed vocabulary expressed the sense of both parties to the contract that the vassal was *entitled* to his feof; it was no longer a benefice, but land with which the vassal was clothed, 'invested', as of right, in return for his services.

In the feudal relationship the whip-hand was with the vassal, not with the lord. The close connexion between homage and investiture is the best illustration of the stranglehold which vassals had over lords. At first the vassal was his lord's man for his life and his lord's life; when either died the land reverted freely to the lord or his heirs. But very soon indeed the lord was compelled to re-grant land only to the heir of the vassal: if he wished to have vassals this was the only way he could secure them. He had, therefore, to acquiesce in the hereditary nature of the feof, which he was the more ready to do as he himself was anxious for land and could normally obtain it only by doing homage and becoming a vassal.

Far more important than the vassal's victory in securing hereditary tenure was his victory in securing the right of holding feofs from more than one lord. How soon this breach in the original military concept of vassalage took place it is hard to say: an authentic case has been found as early as 895. Certainly by the end of the tenth century such multiple allegiances were common: the count of Anjou, vassal of Hugh Capet (below, p. 86), did homage in 975 for another feof which he held of the son of the count of Chartres; twenty years later his successor Fulk Nerra (below, p. 116) who was equally a vassal of the king of France, did homage to William duke of Aquitaine for a feof in Poitou. By the eleventh century many a 'baron' (Fr. *baro*=man) held one feof from another baron, a further feof from a great bishopric, and a third from the king; soon a magnate of any standing was a vassal of more than one lord. This, of course, completely undermined vassalage as a way of securing dependable military service, for a man's masters might be at loggerheads and each claim his sword. An attempt was, indeed, made to secure an overriding loyalty—liege homage —but here again liege homages were soon multiplied. Sometimes, if a lord was particularly anxious to avoid the permanent loss of land or a castle he enfeoffed a servile retainer (*ministerialis*) with it, whose unfree status precluded any pretensions to hereditary right; and at first in such cases the feof remained revocable at will. But tenure by sergeanty (as it was called in England) or the labour-feof (*Dienstlehen*, as it was called in Germany), often only produced a kind of inferior knightly or vassal class.

The hereditary nature of vassalage and the feof never quite obscured their origin in a purely personal contract between a lord and a warrior. The lord received homage when his vassal inherited, the vassal did homage afresh when his lord was succeeded by his heir. If the vassal died leaving a minor as his successor, the feof was administered by the lord till the child came of age; if the vassal was succeeded by an heiress, the lord again administered the lands and bestowed the girl's hand on a suitor. In default of heirs the lands 'escheated' (were forfeited) to the superior. These were valuable rights for the lord, but though they betray the overriding adult masculinity of feof-holding, they were in practice modified: women were soon giving and taking homage; they, no less than the men, were feof-hunters, and both men and women regarded marriage primarily as a means of acquiring territorial possessions.

The relationships created by homage and investiture, and descending in the families of lord and 'man', were dominant in the period between 800 and 1300, but they were not universal. Even in France there were many lands which were held absolutely by their lords, which were not feofs, which (in the technical language of the time) were *allodial*. Only in England, where the Norman conquerors had *tabula rasa* to mark with their systematic rationalization of the French institutions they had so quickly adopted, was there reality in the doctrine 'no land without a lord'.[1] At the other extreme in Germany allodial land was always common; 'feofs held of the sun', as they were termed, could readily be obtained by an energetic knight who struck into the forest, or moved east towards the Slav no-man's-land.

The employment of the vassal-feof arrangement by the governing class ultimately led to the development of a hierarchial theory. The vassal had his lord, who was vassal to some other lord. Such a pyramid culminated in the king and, as we shall see, kings ultimately took advantage of the power which was implicit in this recognition of their superiority. Yet it was to be long before the king was admitted to have much more real power than he could exert effectively, and usually he was able to command

[1] *Allodium* is Latinized from German *Allod*, which seems to have meant 'complete property'. The French have *alleu*, but in English we have no word of our own but must use the Latin, good evidence that the allodium was unknown in England.

the obedience of only the lesser 'tenants-in-chief' or magnates holding their lands directly from him; a great count or duke might theoretically owe fealty to a king but in fact pursued his own policy. Dukes of Normandy were vassals of the French Crown; but after 1066 the duke was sometimes, as king of England, ruler of an independent realm. In any case, as we have noted, feudal relationships were not a neat succession of lords and vassals: many a tenant-in-chief was also a vassal to some lesser lord for part of his estates. Thus as a military instrument feudal obligation was soon ineffective. We can see this in the whittling down of the purely military duties of the vassal. By the end of the eleventh century only forty days of service could be demanded. Beyond that the lord had to pay his vassal. Before long many vassals and lords were glad to compound altogether for military service by paying *scutage*—shield money—and feudalism took a long step towards becoming a mere cloak for the exchange and purchase of land by the free 'military' class. When a great man did homage for land held of a little man it is ludicrous to suppose that any military contract was involved in reality.

Homage and the feof had emerged from the uncertainties of the four centuries before 800, when a strong arm was a man's best protection and claim to advancement. By the twelfth century the noble class had emerged; a categorical difference had arisen between the free knightly or chivalrous class and the unfree peasantry, between the *service* of a noble, and the *servitude* of the workers on his estates. This difference was increasingly reflected in the way of life of the two groups.

The chivalrous class lived, like the peasantry, in the country, though in the south of France and in Italy some nobles built their fortified homes in the old towns. Wooden fortresses on hill-tops (real or artificial) surrounded by palisades, had been all that the first generations of magnates could procure, but by the twelfth century stone castles had arisen in the chief estates of even the lesser lords. In these dour and draughty homes the knight or baron dwelt in a more or less constant state of alert, confined in promiscuous intimacy with his household and retainers, rather like the captain of a small and overloaded ship on an uneasy sea. His provisions were consumed locally and, if he was a man of means, he moved around his manors as he exhausted the supplies at hand. His relaxations partook of the warlike origin of his order; he hunted and played at war in the tournament, so that beasts for the chase and heavy war-horses were an integral and expensive part of his establishment. This life was prepared for in youth. The nobleman normally put his son at an early age into the household of his own chief lord, where the boy learnt to call his future lord Sire or Sir (another derivative of *senior*) and the lady *dame*; at this stage, indeed, the boy saw more of the ladies than of the men—he was a page, or valet. Later, in adolescence, he served the men, attending them in battle, in the hunting-field, at the tournament, and being termed an *esquire* (Lat. *scutarius* = shield-bearer). Finally, when he had served these probationary stages he was dubbed to knighthood, by being hit with a sword over the shoulders; he could now be given his adult military equipment; he 'had his spurs'. He was then a full-blown knight, ready to organize for himself the itinerant life of manor and tourney.

There was, of course, in practice all the difference in the world between the great man, lord of many manors, with numerous sub-vassals and many mighty castles, and the isolated knight who was master only of a small estate and with inadequate resources to maintain him in his station in society. Such social differences were scarcely reflected by the old titles of Carolingian days which had themselves become hereditary. The count had little added status, though a duchy or a marquisate were coveted. Yet in France and Germany, though social distinctions reflected varying wealth, the knightly class on the whole was thoroughly united. The knight could be judged only by his peers (his equals), was a member of a privileged caste. In England such legal privileges were less vital, and gradually only the knights who were summoned to the king's council were termed barons; for the rest the boundary was drawn between noble and serf and every freeman was in law a gentleman. The gulf separating noble and non-noble was wider in continental Europe and there, when money taxes replaced military service as the basis of government, these distinctions were to harden. Knighthood thus became, not merely a socially, but also a fiscally protected position.

The distinction between the freeman of knightly rank and the serf takes us back once more to the social structure of the non-noble rural population. The economic activities of the servile peasantry have already been touched on (above, p. 42). Here we must note that the feudal relationships we have just described were developed most fully in regions where arable farming on the two or three field 'systems' was found, and feudalism is found only in attenuated forms among the hill populations practising run-rig and its equivalents, or among the shepherds of the mountains. The reason for this is clear enough. Land granted as a benefice or feof had necessarily to be land which was tolerably productive, in order to maintain the knight and his entourage. To that extent 'seignorialism' and feudalism are intimately related, though (as we shall notice) the rights of the lord over the land and its peasants did not disappear as genuine feudalism did, but survived in new forms to a much later date.

In the areas of high agriculture and high feudalism the peasants were organized by their masters in manors (Fr. *cour*, Ger. *Hof*), which were at once economic and administrative units, the lord being both 'a managing director and a commander'. In both capacities he acted through an agent and only on the smaller estates did he participate directly in the affairs of his lands. His agent was often chosen from among the personal retainers of servile status in his own retinue; often he was one of the serfs in the manor; in either case the post usually became hereditary and the reeve or bailiff, as he was called (Lat. *villicus, major*, Fr. *maire*, Ger. *Bauermeister*) was rewarded by a rake-off. The bailiff had to supervise the day-to-day working of the manorial economy. This involved the performance by the serfs of compulsory work on the land held by the lord under his direct control and of various other services. The lord's portion of the manor was termed the 'demesne' (*terra indominicata*, the land under the lord) and it was normally scattered in strips, among the servile holdings, in the open fields. On the demesne the serfs of the manor had to labour each year for a number of days fixed locally by custom. In addition the lord was paid regularly certain fixed dues, in cash or in kind, by each serf with a holding of his own; and the serf with his family was required to perform certain manufacturing duties—notably the weaving of cloth from flax or wool provided by the lord.

These economic rights were extensive enough, but they were at every point reinforced by the lord's right to command, to administer justice, and raise armed forces from among his serfs. To the exercise of these quasi-public functions, which, from at least the Carolingian period, were associated with lordship of land, may be attributed the *banalités* (*ban*= summons or command): the peasant was compelled to bring his grain to the lord's watermill, to bring his apples and grapes to his lord's press, his flour to his lord's oven—in all cases paying for the privilege. Equally the lord as a chieftain could insist on the performance of extra services on the demesne or on building work, though in such cases he had to pay a reward or wage. In the long run the right to tax or tallage (Fr. *tailler*) his serfs was the main symbol of the lord's public rights, together with his judicial administration—also an important source of revenue; though the tallage was in practice, like the law administered in the manorial court, regulated by custom.

The villagers managed and administered by reeve or *maire*, were nearly all of servile status. The service they owed was, unlike that rendered by vassal to superior, inescapable. But from manor to manor, from one part of Europe to another, an infinite variety characterizes the servile relationship. Every kind of economic and social subjection is found from slavery, and conditions akin to it, to freedom and relative freedom. What is impressive, however, is not such a diversity (historically to be expected, since the land was worked both by men whose ancestors had been real slaves, the chattels imported by Roman legions and German war bands, and by others descended from the yeoman tenantry of free villages), but the tendency for the peasantry to approximate to a norm of servitude. In this respect nothing is more suggestive than the fate of the word 'villein' or villain, originally a term (*villanus*) describing one of the comparatively free classes of peasants. The inevitability of the progress to servile subjection may also be seen in the Byzantine Empire, where free villages and a free peasantry survived for long under imperial protection, but at last fell more or less into line with western Christendom.

Servitude was undoubtedly a harsh condition: the serf could not marry (at any rate outside the manor) without his lord's permission; he could not leave the manor, or inherit his father's holding, without the consent of his lord; and on these occasions he payed a fine. Such controls were naturally resented. Yet the relationship we have been considering had compensations. Serfdom, to begin with, was not slavery. The serf had a right to his holding, he had a family which could inherit it and was, in practice, not at the mercy of his lord. A few real slaves were there, whose status served to stress the relative security of the serf, but these were all non-Christian; the very word itself was derived from Slav prisoners, and owed its currency to those imported through Dalmatia in the

THE STRUCTURE OF SOCIETY

thirteenth century.[1] Moreover the lord had no social or economic inducement to maltreat his servile tenants. The land he possessed was useless without their labour; in an economy designed to produce a sufficiency rather than a surplus there was little incentive to exploitation. Nor were the peasantry in the ninth and tenth centuries separated from their masters by an unbridgeable gulf of convention. The peasant's way of life was for long not vastly different from his master's. Both lived on a narrow economic margin; the lord's house and the peasant's hovel would today be regarded as almost equally squalid, both being overcrowded, insanitary, and comfortless. In war no doubt the lord was better able to protect himself, but his ampler and more permanent accommodation was in part designed to give asylum to the men and cattle on his land. To pestilence lord and man were almost equally vulnerable, and in famine the peasant, though no doubt subjected to great pressure by the bailiff, had his cache of grain which it would not be easy to unearth.

These stabilizing factors go far to account for the marked absence of social disturbances in the early Middle Ages. There were no doubt isolated occasions when serfs combined to resist a brutal master; many of the incidental privileges of the lord were characterized as 'evil customs'. But the monastic chronicles have little to tell us of peasant risings before 1250, and this is good evidence, for the monasteries were extensive landlords and the monks extremely jealous

[1] *Sclavus* = slave (rather than Slav) is first found in the tenth century as a result of the trade in Slavs captured in the German expansion eastwards; they were sold mainly to Moslems in Spain. This trade and the word itself disappear in the early eleventh century to reappear later.

of their rights. It is highly significant that almost the only examples of serious agrarian trouble earlier than the fourteenth century are due to a few attempts to destroy unruly and rapacious barons made by the peasantry under clerical leadership and in support of the Church's campaign for peace (below, p. 127); such a rising occurred, for example, near Bourges in 1038. Yet the pitchfork is an effective weapon against a mounted man and it is hardly conceivable that the warrior class could have effortlessly dominated greatly superior numbers of peasants for five centuries if the latter had been fired by deep-seated grievances.

The five centuries ending with the thirteenth were, of course, centuries of change on the manor just as they were in the feof, and as these changes were mainly favourable to the serf, we have here a further explanation of his acquiescence in a way of life which was unquestionably hard. The serf of the ninth century differed from the serf of the late twelfth in that at the later date his services were much less onerous and his money payments much more so than they had been earlier. Instead of labouring on his lord's demesne for perhaps as many as a hundred days in the year he now had to work only for eight or ten; instead of the *corvées de fabrication*, the peasant and his family were paid for weaving done at home. At the same time the twelfth and thirteenth centuries witness a widespread writing down of customs and as they were committed to paper there was nearly always an amelioration in their terms. No single explanation covers this important development. We have already noticed a steady rise in population and an attack on the

THE STRUCTURE OF SOCIETY 61

waste; a lord could only retain his serfs by making conditions more attractive at a time when he and other lords were seeking to extend the area of cultivation. From the peasant's point of view, the family-holding in any manor tended to get smaller and smaller as it was progressively divided among the serf's heirs and there was thus every inducement for younger sons to strike out for even distant areas of new settlement, or for the slowly expanding urban communes. These towns will be discussed later, at a point when they change the whole pattern of society (below, p. 147); but they were the product of an increasing commercial activity which, together with the rising population and the *morcellement* of the serf's holding, combined to transform the lord into a *rentier*.

The lord turned increasingly to commercial sources to satisfy his needs; commerce rose in order to satisfy the requirements of a knightly class which was slowly becoming more refined and less bellicose. Here cause and effect were inextricably combined and everything urged the lord to secure money rather than services from his peasants in order to make his purchases. This turn in events might at first sight seem to bear heavily on the peasantry. But in fact the peasants were able to profit from an expansion in the volume of money transactions sooner than their masters. The lord lived off a fixed income of goods and services; the peasant could often produce a surplus for sale from his own lands. The elasticity in manorial productivity lay, in fact, not in the demesne, but in the servile holdings, and serfs were thus in a position to meet the lord when he demanded money payments rather than services. The demesne itself was soon severely reduced and farmed out by the lords; in certain cases it disappeared altogether. By the thirteenth century the lord was living mainly off the money produced by his manors.

By the close of the thirteenth century the services performed by the peasant population in western Christendom had been sensibly reduced and in places they had virtually disappeared. Instead a great deal of money changed hands. The lord's ancient right of tallage was now more important than ever before; the serfs were really rent-paying tenants; and the tithe collected for the support of parish and diocesan clergy also often found its way into the lord's pocket. The members of the knightly class, thus endowed, now embarked on a way of life which soon sharply distinguished them from the humble villagers. Castles become much larger and are handsomely plenished; the number of rooms multiply; exotic clothes and daintier food characterize the nobility. In such a situation it only needed economic regression to throw the economic machinery hopelessly out of gear. This was in fact to happen in the fourteenth century (below, p. 172), with all the concomitant venom of social dissension and class war. It would be folly to suppose the peasants were 'happy' in a 'golden middle age' before this happened. But between 800 and 1300 the two great groups of lords and peasants were, roughly speaking, content with their lots. The changing social pattern reflected an improvement in the condition of both knight and serf.

The above description of society has accepted the distinction made at the time between the free warrior class and the unfree serf class. Certainly from

THE STRUCTURE OF SOCIETY 63

a social point of view only two classes can be seen. There was, however, another group in the community, the Church and its clergy, numerous, well-organized, and inspired by a coherent ambition. If such a group existed, should it not form a third element in society, distinguished alike from the knights devoted to war and administration of land, and from the peasants, unfree, tied by manorial obligation, manual labourers of the soil?

Later on such a tripartite division was accepted and developed: the clerk prayed, the knight fought, the peasant worked, each accomplishing his God-given role in the community. Yet such a picture would be false of the period we are at present considering. The clergy were, indeed, too closely involved at every point in secular affairs to be able to maintain so distinct a place in society. For the Church was immensely wealthy in the only wealth that mattered, land. This territorial endowment of the Church goes back to the Roman Empire. It was vastly accelerated in the troubled years of the invasions and settlement, for then, and later, when more order prevailed, the gift of lands to the clergy was the readiest contribution a magnate could make to the Christian cause. Piety drove the laity to endowment: what other reparation could an illiterate and often superstitious class make for their sins on earth? But generosity was sometimes tinged with self-interest. The church or monastery which a magnate had endowed was, in some sense, the property of his family, where he might reasonably seek shelter and entertainment, where his younger sons might reasonably expect preferment and where (in the case of a female convent) his womenfolk might retire. Such alienations of land were, of course, in perpetuity. While this had the advantage that they did not become the hereditary property of a land-grabbing vassal, it also meant that they ceased to flow in feudal circulation. Later such gifts into the dead hand of the Church (Eng. 'mortmain', Fr. *mainmorte*) were more or less limited by the common consent of the magnates. But in the four or five centuries before 1300 the donation of lands to the Church had reached tremendous proportions. The kings of Germany had, in particular, been quick to see the possibilities of using the bishop and the abbot as makeweights against the lesser baronage and as barriers against the eastern Slavs. Great sees were established at Cologne, Hamburg, and Magdeburg, and many lesser prelates looked to their secular patrons as secular lords.

Bishoprics and abbeys established in this way readily fell into the pattern of feudalism and so did the less heavily endowed but older sees which existed in the Romanized parts of Europe. The king, or sometimes another great magnate, appointed his nominee as bishop and, if the abbots of the Benedictine houses (which were now spread thickly over Christendom) were sometimes more canonically elected, local lords usually exercised a predominant part in the lay affairs of the houses as their 'advocates' or secular administrators and protectors. One cannot therefore be surprised that many of the higher clergy were mighty warriors themselves, responding to their feudal responsibilities so thoroughly that their priestly functions were forgotten. Bruno, archbishop of Cologne during the tenth century, was a trusted imperial commander and

THE STRUCTURE OF SOCIETY 65

needed his military talents also to administer his duchy of Lorraine; in the following century Archbishop Pilgrim, also of Cologne, commanded an imperial army. The higher clergy were equally involved in feudal relationships as masters of land; they too had their vassals, and if they could not demand aid for the knighting of their sons or the endowment of their marriageable daughters, there were other financial stresses which a vassal of the Church had often to meet—payment for the bishop's visit to Rome, for example, or the repair of the cathedral.

The smallest unit in the Church, the parish, was also intimately connected with lordship and land. Over most of Europe the parish church was built and endowed by the local lord of the manor. The parish priest was ordained and inducted by the higher clergy; but he was appointed by the lord who possessed the advowson (Lat. *advocatio*), the gift of the living and who regarded the village church simply as his property; after all the endowment of the priest was a proportion (usually called a tenth or tithe, though often less than that in practice) of the produce of the lord's manor and a plot of village land (the glebe). Many parishes had, it is true, been established by bishops and abbots in the early days on Church lands. But this did not mean that the incumbents were treated any differently or that these churches were less 'proprietory'.

From the poor parish priest to the powerful bishop or abbot, clergy were thus closely associated with the secular order of the day. True, they were in a sense legally separated from their non-tonsured fellows: from the point of view of discipline a clergyman was subjected to his own officers, the secular clergy to bishop and archbishop, the monk to his abbot and his Order. But the social bonds of land were a separate and potent control. A bishop swore homage to the great man who had appointed him and as often as not the prince invested him not only with the symbols of his territorial lordship but with the ring and staff of his spiritual charge. Even little lords sometimes received homage from their parish priests. From high to low there was an assimilation of the prelate's office to the vassal's fief. As we shall notice, this was to cause conflict when the Church sought to remedy some of the abuses which were naturally associated with the processes of secular control.

Yet the Church as a whole never lost its sense of mission. Individual popes and priests were sometimes corrupt and ignorant beyond any present-day comparison, and the disease of worldly wealth had obscured for many a prelate the other-wordliness of his profession. If such brutish figures had been general the chroniclers would, however, have had less to say of them, the laity would not have endowed religious foundations and the clergy themselves would have had no impetus to reform old institutions and create new ones. Such a flowering of Christian organizations as we see in the tenth, eleventh, and twelfth centuries is sufficient evidence that religion was lively. We may note too that spiritual innovations, like the social innovations of feudalism, are closely connected with north France and Burgundy.

In 910 a duke of Aquitaine founded a Benedictine house at Cluny near Macon. Under a series of able, original, and long-lived abbots Cluny developed along lines which were novel and were to prove infectious.

Having secured immunity from the control of the local bishop, the abbot retained control over the daughter-houses which rapidly multiplied. The priors of these houses also met from time to time in general congregations at the mother-house, and strict discipline was constantly refreshed by visits of the abbot in person. Slackness had at first no place in the Cluniac Order; the Benedictine rule was rigorously enforced. Many other houses voluntarily submitted to Cluny and others were stimulated to a similar reform.

Cluny was, in a sense, no more than a Benedictine renaissance. Other inventions were in some ways farther removed from the original rule of St. Benedict. At Cîteaux, also in Burgundy, a new Order was founded in 1098. The Cistercians sought simplicity, a withdrawal from the world of man, and manual as opposed to intellectual labour. Their plain buildings arose in remote valleys and on windswept moors. Cîteaux never had great abbots like Cluny: but in Bernard (*d.* 1153), abbot of the daughter-house of Clairvaux, it had the advantage of a personality who dominated his age. St. Bernard, the denouncer of slack popes and temporizing kings, the preacher from whom women hid their menfolk lest they deserted the hearth for the cloister, whose message captivated a French prince into his Order, whose advice was so constantly sought by the great men of his day that he was frequently taken away from his beloved community, typifies the urgency and the austerity of the monastery. Renunciation was his message. Laughter he abominated. His favourite text came from St. Jerome: 'A monk's duty is to mourn, not to teach.' The monk took upon himself a large share of the world's sin and in his isolation cultivated a purity and single-mindedness which was clearly impossible in day-to-day life in the world.

Such a renunciation of the world's way was even more strongly marked in another Order, the Carthusians, so named from the mother-house in the Grande-Chartreuse near Grenoble (1084). The 'Charterhouses' of this Order were really groups of hermit cells. The Order maintained its early strictness and continued to enjoy public support long after this had been withdrawn from the regular clergy as a whole. Two orders of 'regular canons' must also be mentioned. These were the Augustinians (eleventh century) and the Premonstratensians (1120). At first both concerned themselves with the performance of parochial duties, unlike the cloistered religious, though the Augustinians later abandoned this and became more like ordinary monks.

The monastery was a familiar sight in the landscape of Europe. The cathedrals, many of which survive today, were also beginning by the twelfth century to rear their tremendous spires and pinnacles. The parish churches dotted over the country-side were even more insistent reminders of the relevance of religion. It was a world of bells, tolling monastic hours, ringing in great peals from the towers of minsters and cathedrals, with calm regularity in the villages. The priest baptized, married, and buried his parishioners. The parish church was a familiar and friendly spot round which much local life revolved. How strongly pagan superstition lingered on as a source of religious awe we can never know: local saints were sometimes related to earlier deities of fountain, wood, and hill. But the calendar of the

Church permeated ancient winter and spring festivals with a new magic. Christmas and Easter were tremendous occasions, when lord and serf alike shared the drama of the Incarnation and the Passion, learning little perhaps from the Latin service, but much from the painted decorations on the wall and the stylized ritual of the clergy.

Socially, none the less, the clergy fall into much the same divisions as the laity. True, the hierarchy connected all the religious in a common chain of obedience. A distant pope in Rome communicated with archbishops themselves placed above the bishops in their provinces. The bishop, surrounded by a 'family' of clerics, responsible for the teaching and ordaining of priests, and for the discipline of many of the monks in his diocese as well as of all the secular clergy, was also a judge of clerical offenders and of certain offences in general (matrimony and wills, for instance). The bishop controlled his diocese through one or more archdeacons, below whom certain parish clergy were appointed as rural deans. Finally, at the foot of the ladder, were the ordinary priests and monks.

Yet at all times in the period discussed in this book a great gulf separated the little priest from the grand prelate, greater in its way than that separating the lord from his servile dependents. In theory all priests were given a respect above that accorded by laity to other laity, but the abbot of a great house or the bishop of a wealthy diocese were not only protected by their cloth, they were all too often related to the magnates around them by blood. Family connexions had often secured such men their promotion and, as prelates and nobles frequently met one another, the social outlook of both groups tended to be identical. 'Haute église requiert hautesce', writes a poet about 1210: great prelates should be nobles; and Church law in fact declared that a man of servile origin should not be ordained as a priest. In practice, however, the lower clergy was recruited almost exclusively from men who were only technically 'free', and a chasm of convention separated the important clergyman from his humble colleague in the small parish. The latter was drawn from peasant stock, and his remuneration was so small that he often had to labour on the glebe like a tenant-farmer, accepting, more often than not, the solaces of the village—a wife or mistress and the ale-house. Poor men could rise to the very summit of the hierarchy; Pope Gregory VII was a peasant's son. This was nevertheless most exceptional. Popes, bishops, and abbots were normally of gentle birth and the man of the commons who rose in the Church was often ill-received by the great magnates with whom he had to associate. 'Your father and mother were villeins', Joinville told Louis IX's almoner Robert de Sorbon in front of the whole court, 'yet you have abandoned the vesture worn by them and wear richer woollen cloth than the King himself.' Such rudeness betrays the nobleman's profound dislike for non-noble prelates and we gather that this sentiment was shared by the more tactful Louis. The poor monk was in a somewhat different case. His poverty was individual and voluntary, enjoined on him by his Order which might itself be vastly well-endowed. From the start, moreover, the cloister had attracted men of knightly rank, and this may perhaps be seen in the title 'dominus' applied to the Benedictine monk. And in the eleventh and twelfth centuries many bishops were chosen from monasteries, thus entering, often re-entering, the ranks of the potentates.

The Church, then, was socially at one with the order of lay society. Permeated by feudalism from its vast landed endowment, divided into magnates and small fry, like the secular world, it represented an aspiration towards the creation of a distinct element in society rather than the achievement of this aim. It is, indeed, hard to see how the way of renunciation could have been compatible with a success greater than that accorded to the clergy in the eleventh to thirteenth centuries. Religion was, surely, never more actual in day-to-day affairs than it was then. In western Christendom there were no unbelievers except the tiny Jewish communities living on sufferance and at the mercy of unpredictable persecution; and there were virtually no heretics. All men acknowledged the superior character of the clerical order. But this pervading sense of religion was itself expressed in forms which underlined social distinctions. All men were equal before God, yet if a donation to the Church was an act of merit, the rich founder of an abbey might clearly be better off hereafter than the poor man who could not spare anything for the saints. Christian doctrine in the West had, certainly, a potent influence on society. From Roman times onwards it had been a bitter enemy to the slavery of Christians. It strove with all its might to substitute trial by ordeal for the less regulated and bloodier duel and family vengeance. Later it had tried to humanize the feudal relationship itself. The growth of chivalrous attitudes in the late eleventh century and after was largely due to clerical influence: the sword which was used to dub a knight was blessed by a priest, and it became common for the esquire to spend the night preceding his 'ordination' as a chevalier in a vigil of prayer. 'Courtesy' (*courtoisie* = a courtly way of life) similarly owed much to Christian teaching, and the substitution of loyalty to an ideal, rather than to a feudal lord, did much to soften the harshness of life in noble households. Yet these ameliorations, it must be observed, mainly affected the knightly class and spilled over into the conscience of common men in the less desirable forms of Mariolatry and saint worship.

That we are able to discern the general pattern of society at all is, of course, due to the Church. Literacy was almost completely restricted to the clergy and the written memorials of this age are, with few exceptions, due to them. The clergy wrote and spoke Latin. While this was anything but a dead language, it was the language of only a handful of experts surrounded by a vernacular-speaking majority. These vernaculars, which daily influenced Latin farther and farther away from the 'classical' language, were not learnt: 'learning' meant only Latin learning. The knightly class, of course, spoke their local vernacular and in it epic stories of war and prowess were recited by wandering bards to fill the idle hours of winter in the castles. From the eleventh century many of these began to be written down, like the most famous of them, the *Song of Roland*. Later on, and mirroring the changed sentiment we have noted, these rhymed epics gave way more and more to romantic tales such as the Arthurian cycle and to the lyrical poetry of courtly love. The day-to-day acts of administration and government (apart from those in the Church itself) were also normally conducted in the vernaculars, but they were recorded almost always in the Latin of the clerks who wrote them down—in the charters (*carta, cartula* = a piece of paper) confirming legal actions such as alienations of lands or public alliances between princes, and in the chronicles composed by the monastic historians. Even the ephemeral vernacular literature of relaxation was more often than not written down by a priest so that we perforce regard the whole period through clerical spectacles.

If secular literature was transmitted by the clergy it goes without saying that the scholarship and science of the Middle Ages were almost solely cultivated by Churchmen. The use of Latin for services meant that 'grammar' was part of a priest's necessary equipment. With it went two other subjects equally derived from antiquity, 'rhetoric' or prose style and 'dialectic' or logic. This group was the *trivium* which, with the more advanced subjects of the *quadrivium* (music, astronomy, geometry, arithmetic), formed the 'seven liberal arts' of the medieval school. In practice the *trivium* was the normal fare of the monastery school, where novices were trained, and of the bishop's school where candidates for ordination received instruction. The monastic school did not develop as did the bishop's school. From 1179 every diocese was required by Church law to provide a schoolmaster to teach without charge, and even earlier than this some episcopal schools had masters whose fame drew students from far afield. Men travelled to Chartres for literature, to Laon for philosophy, to Montpellier for medicine. After instruction they were in their turn given a licence to teach by the bishop or his chancellor, they became 'masters of arts'.

The twelfth century witnessed a flowering of this instruction which culminated in the emergence of guilds of masters (*universitas* = a corporation) who organized themselves so that they could control teaching and the conferring of degrees and thus become more or less independent of the bishop. An independent school grew up at Paris during the last quarter of the twelfth century, after two generations of great teachers (including Abelard) had made the city famous for its teaching in arts and in the new 'theology'. Soon similar great schools (*studia generalia*) grew up—as at Oxford and Cambridge—conferring on their graduates the right to teach everywhere, the *jus ubique docendi*. A similar development is found at exactly the same time in Italy, though there the first schools were predominantly lay and had even more ancient origins. At Salerno medicine was taught; at Bologna law, both Roman and Canon. Medicine and law attracted an older type of student and at Bologna the original guilds were formed, not by the teachers, but by the students.[1] The Bologna-type of university also soon produced rivals, Reggio, Vicenza, and Padua being among the first.

In all universities instruction by the teacher consisted in commenting on an accepted text. Thus Donatus was a basic authority in grammar, part of Aristotle (translated by Boethius) in logic, and in

[1] Who organized themselves in 'nations' according to their country of origin. 'Nations' are also found in the large faculties of arts in the Paris-type of university.

theology the standard text of the Bible (the Vulgate) with collections (*summae*) of comments, the most famous of which was that compiled by Peter Lombard. In law Justinian's collections (above, pp. 7–8) were similarly glossed,[1] while collections of papal decretals culminating in Gratian's (below, p. 95) formed the basis of the study of Canon law.

The Church naturally took a lively interest in these developments so largely inspired by her needs. By the mid-thirteenth century it was firmly established that the *studia generalia* or universities fell directly within the purview of the pope. All students were clergy, at least in minor orders, and thus exempt from control by secular courts. The danger lay in the unexpected twists of unfettered speculation. Already in the mid-twelfth century Abelard's systematic logic had incurred the violent persecution of St. Bernard, and by the end of the century the great controversy on 'universals' had arisen. This seemingly innocuous debate, on whether abstract concepts—'humanity' or 'justice'—could be said to have an independent existence, provoked violent polemics, the 'Nominalists' arguing that such concepts were mere mental categories, the 'Realists' that they were valid realities. Yet clearly the issue of the argument might affect the whole development of Christian belief and the papacy, as well as the contending philosophers, scrutinized each argument with a new concern for orthodoxy (below, p. 213).

More immediately important than these advances in education and learning was the sharing by all students of certain basic assumptions which not only

[1] The gloss or commentary was written round the relevant portion of the text.

coloured thought but which were accepted by all—laity as well as clergy—as representing a true picture of the universe. Derived in the last resort from Platonic and Neo-Platonic sources, reinforced by elements in Hebrew and Christian thought, this concept of the cosmos fitted neatly enough the stratifications of lay society, the pyramid of clerical ranks and offices, and the nature of the physical world as then known. The whole created universe was regarded as a vast ladder of ascending entities running unbroken from the edge of Hell to the infinite and ultimate unity of God. In this divinely appointed order each individual object or concept was both part of some greater whole and itself a microcosm of inferior creation: in either aspect it was integrally involved in the 'Great Chain of Being'. In this series, man held a critical place: half spiritual, his soul linked him with the heavenly orders stretching upwards to God; half animal, his body placed him over 'the fish of the sea, and over the fowl of the air, and over all the earth, and over every creeping thing that creepeth upon the earth'. From such an organization of the whole of experience derived the acceptance of what seem to us somewhat strange analogies. It was possible to argue from one part of the cosmic hierarchy to another; to define the relations of father to family or of pope to emperor, from the superiority of the heart to the limbs or the sun to the moon. And once such a correspondence had been established it had all the compulsion of eternal and inescapable truth.

In view of the controlling hand which the clergy had in the transmission of our documents and of the part played by concepts of hierarchy and order in all speculation, it is even more impressive that the dominance of secular values in society stands out as clearly as it does. And though much that was purely clerical in inspiration was to have a long and fruitful influence in later ages (as, for instance, the 'Great Chain of Being' itself, which lingered on as a mode of thought until the seventeenth century and later), the patterns of lay action engraved themselves even more indelibly on the future.

West European peoples pay tribute to this when they continue to speak the language of feudal relationships. In English we address our letters to 'Esquire' and call strangers and persons in authority 'Sir'; in French *Monsieur* and in Italian *Signore*, hark back to *senior* or 'lord', which in its Latin form of *dominus* has given us monastic 'dom' and Spanish (and academic) 'don'; in German the word *Herr* is equally derived from the feudal lord. 'Benefice', as applied to clerical appointments, tells its own story; so does the word 'prebend' when we recall that it is cognate with the word 'provender'. But perhaps we should ponder more deeply the evolution of 'service' and 'servitude'. In classical Latin the words from which they were ultimately developed had only the sense of a servile and unworthy status. It is because of the structure of society considered earlier in this chapter that 'service' finally acquired its honourable connotation, for it was associated with feudal service, the voluntary obligations of one free man to another; and the service of God in church was a further influence in the same direction. 'Servitude' came to have a depreciatory sense as a result of its connexion with subjection, with the *servus* or serf, tied to the land and manual labour: and this despite the papal formula, *servus servorum Dei* (above, p. 28). At the time, however, so abrupt an antithesis was only implicit. It was in and after the fourteenth century (below, p. 174), that the distinction became harsh and inescapable: service for the few and servitude for the many.

CHAPTER IV

LAW AND GOVERNMENT:
THE CUSTODY OF CHRISTENDOM

Survival of Roman influences; but triumph of customary law; and survival of kingship; the German Emperor and the Church; Church reform and papal leadership; Gregory VII and investiture; imperium *and* sacerdotium, *growth of papal claims; the unity of Christendom.*

IN the previous chapter we have isolated the main social groups in Europe during the four central centuries of the Middle Ages. It was almost inevitable that such a picture should be rather timeless. In turning in this chapter and the next to the problems of government and law in this period we shall be able to see that society was in fact anything but static, and we shall also have occasion (in discussing monarchy) to note the emergence of a group in the community distinct in certain respects from the landed magnates as a whole.

The Romans had in some ways succeeded in diffusing their values more widely after the end of the Empire than during its existence. The barbarian settlers were only a small conquering group spread over populations which had often been Romanized for a dozen generations or more. It was hardly surprising that in France, Spain, and Italy the new masters soon spoke the language of their subjects, albeit in the debased forms which were to lead to French, Spanish, and Italian. In absorbing the language the victors absorbed much else besides and the process of 'Romanization' was encouraged by a ready acceptance of Roman Christianity. Such literature as there was derived largely from Roman inspiration. The clerks were no doubt partly responsible for that, as they were for the survival of classical motifs in the limited fine art of the Dark Ages. Even the architecture is appropriately described in English as 'Romanesque'. These cultural values were exported from the 'Romance' countries to the purely Teutonic lands beyond the Rhine and over the Channel. Yet there were two fields in which Rome had been pre-eminent and in which the barbarians completely reversed Roman conceptions: law and government. For a Roman law was the edict of central government, rational, written, and systematized, while government was (at any rate in theory) the responsibility of the senate and people of Rome, or of their chief magistrate, the emperor. After the settlement of the barbarians there was a general acceptance of law as unwritten custom, and government was felt, however vaguely, to be the responsibility of kings.

Customary law had been known to the Romans, for they dealt with many primitive peoples who determined social penalties in a gathering of elders where a king or priest acted as the mouthpiece of tradition. But the written edict of Rome was regarded in the Empire as superior to customary law, when the two came into conflict. After invasion was over, the tribal law of the German intruders became fixed by the areas in which they dwelt—became, to use the technical language of later days, 'territorialized', so that men asked a stranger not, 'To what folk do you belong?' but 'Where do you come from?' Since the majority of even the masters in some areas were 'Roman', the 'custom' of such an area was 'Roman' law. Yet even in such areas custom prevailed over the codified edicts though (as we shall see) the survival of a potentially more sophisticated jurisprudence was to have important consequences later on. We must also not be misled by the survival of so-called codes of laws of early barbarian kings. These were pathetic imitations of Roman ways and, like Carolingian 'capitularies' or general edicts, peter out in the ninth century. The 'laws' of a king are the customs confirmed by a king. As has been often said, there is no *legislation* in the Middle Ages proper, the place of law-making in modern society being taken by the interpretation of custom. Custom prevailed equally in the smaller political units, determining the precise duties involved in vassalage in any given area, and regulating the rights of the lord and his serfs in the manor. Just as the king could not legislate, so the relationships of a lord to his free vassals and of the seigneur to his servile tenants were tempered by tradition and lacked a sense of autocratic power. We consequently find a universal fear of creating precedents at all levels in the early Middle Ages, for an unusual action could readily constitute a fresh and perhaps unwelcome 'custom'.

In the field of monarchy, the Romans had already gone some way towards accepting kingship: the later emperors were more and more remote, basing their power on an almost Oriental sense of despotism. But the word *rex*, king, was always suspect to a Roman. It suggested the Tarquins and the dark oppression of the pre-republican period. Even under the Empire the machinery of the senate was maintained and the Empire was, in theory, only an extraordinary magistracy, the fiction being finally developed that the people (by the *lex regia*) had surrendered their power to the *princeps*. After the settlement, as with law, so with monarchy, there was a change. Whatever the position of kings may have been among the Germans before the invasions it was vastly important once they were established in the Empire. Although, as we have noticed, the rulers of the barbarians sought titles such as 'patrician' and 'consul' from Byzantium, they remained kings and *rex* becomes respectable. The emperor at Constantinople was in a sense head of the Christian Church on earth. The barbarian kings were also closely associated with religious practices. Kingship among the barbarians was, indeed, as much a form of priesthood as empire among the Romans was a form of civil magistracy. What made a man a king among the Germans? His descent from a royal family, his acceptance by the important men of the tribe, his hallowing as a leader. These three elements under their later names, hereditary descent, 'election', and consecration, were to remain the basis of monarchy throughout the Middle Ages. True, it was as a leader in war that the king acquired his political power. While successful, disposing of booty and conquered lands, he was richer and more to be feared than any rival, and better able to buy support and pay for services. But his authority, his legitimacy, his very claim to be a leader at all, were due to his being the son of a king, chosen by his people, and made sacred by the Church. These were the sources of the king's divinity.

The barbarian kings were obviously less effective rulers in many ways than the emperors, of whom Roman jurists taught that 'their will has the force of law'. As administrators and legislators they could scarcely be said to exist at all. Though, as we have seen, they tried at first to maintain some administrative machinery, this proved impossible as mobile wealth dried up and revenue from tolls and taxes disappeared; a bureaucracy on the Roman model needed to be paid and, as rewards could only be made from the intermittent spoils of war and from the king's lands, such a bureaucracy was naturally beyond their means. As for legislation, the king was the interpreter of custom determined by the elders and by the great men of the folk in formal gatherings.

Even Charlemagne's vast Empire was run on these primitive lines. The very size of his Empire, it is true, prevented all but a section of the greater magnates from attending the periodical meetings of warriors, the May Fields, but this merely intensified the social weakness of the smaller free men and increased the latent power of the lord of many lands. Government was in the hands of counts ruling in the Emperor's name over counties, and of margraves or marquises responsible for border provinces (marks or marches); but these officers were remote from day-to-day control, despite the imperial legates (*missi dominici*) who were intended to supervise them, and they often acquired personal power in the exercise of their duties. Compared with the welter of contending principalities which had preceded the rise of the Franks and with the chaos which followed their collapse, the Empire of Charles the Great was coherent and well governed, leaving memories of grandeur which are reflected not only in epic literature but also in the rudimentary propaganda of the smaller kings of later days in France, Germany, and England. But intrinsically the centralization attempted by Charles was modest and its practical effect small. A world of custom had no room in it for genuine autocracy; when in the very act of rewarding his followers the king had to deprive himself of land he could only remain wealthy by further conquest—and that, too, increased the wealth of the magnates who shared in the spoils.

In the late Empire the great landowner had normally been also a magistrate; after the barbarian settlement the magnates emerged with legal control over their dependent tenants. The 'free' tenantry were at first to some extent recognized in the systems of family vengeance inherited from earlier German custom: they had a higher blood-price and were judged by their peers (or equals) in the village, hundred,[1] or county court. But the shadowy authority of the Carolingian kings was largely achieved by conferring power over the free men on counts and dukes. As the Carolingian kingdom disintegrated the weak monarchs of the ninth century tried to obtain support by granting individuals immunity from this remnant of public control. Gradually the legal control of the population in an area fell to the magnate who dominated it. In this

[1] This administrative unit, found in Germany and in lands of Teutonic settlement, was latterly (as in England) a territorial subdivision of the county.

way the social distinction between the knightly or land-holding class and the dependent peasant was reflected in the forms of law, gradually transcending kinship, though blood relationship and family loyalties were for long potent elements in both crime and punishment. As far as the knightly class itself was concerned, the machinery of vassalage was itself the law. The custom of feudal tenure in a locality was maintained in the lord's *curia* or court, and there the vassals were judged by their peers. Penalties for offences, which had at first been mainly money compositions, tended to become more violent in the period of the last invasions of the Danes and Magyars; among the magnates trial by battle, the 'judicial duel', was a common form of settling disputes and, as we have seen, the feudal right to defiance was really an appeal to arms.

In this situation an invitation was clearly extended to an enterprising magnate to turn the heterogeneous powers he held into a coherent principality. As a feudal lord he could strive to knit together by the bonds of vassalage the gentry in his vicinity; he could claim to inherit, as a count, marquis, or duke, the administration of such public law as remained—the right to call out the host, control highways, mint money. To this universal attempt to turn control over land into government, or immunity from government (which was the same thing) there was, however, a check. In so far as the independent count or duke, or even the lesser baron, sought to monopolize the public rights which of old had been attached to the king's control over free men, he was paying silent tribute to the principle of monarchy. Moreover, as himself a lord of vassals he accepted a relationship within the land-holding class which again ultimately culminated in the king. The king was thus recognized as supreme lawgiver and supreme lord of land even when his rights in these respects were flouted. Given favourable circumstances an energetic ruler could make much of these influences, as when in 1066 a Norman claimant to the English throne acquired astonishingly wide powers over a large country. Elsewhere the rise of monarchy was less dramatic and, though the residual powers we have touched on here played their part, for most of the time the king owed his authority to the respect which was paid to his office, however weak the individual ruler might be, and to the ability he showed as a magnate to acquire more and more lands under his direct control. These factors may be seen at work in the case of France and Germany.

In 888 the magnates in France broke with the Carolingian line. Charles the Bald's son, Charles the Simple, was aged eight, and in his place Eudes, count of Paris, was chosen as king. This desertion of the old dynasty was not unanimous at the time, and from 893 onwards Eudes had to fight the supporters of Charles the Simple, who was generally recognized as king when Eudes died in 898. In 922 there was fresh trouble and the rebels elected Eudes' brother Robert and, when Robert died in 923, his brother-in-law Raoul, duke of Burgundy. On the death of Raoul, the magnates again reverted to a Carolingian, Charles the Simple's son Louis IV d'Outremer being recalled in 936; and Louis was followed in due course by his son and his grandson. But when the latter died in 987, the magnates elected as king the grandson of Robert, count of Paris, Hugh Capet, who was able successfully to repress the attempt to secure the throne made by another son of Louis IV, Charles, duke of Lower Lorraine. From 987 to 1328 the Capetian dynasty ruled France in direct hereditary succession and the change made in that year to the Valois kings was equally in strict obedience to the law of hereditary descent. The very struggles of the magnates baldly summarized in this paragraph bear witness both to their anxiety that the throne should not remain vacant and to their earnest desire to find a king from the family of a king. It is very remarkable that, however independent a magnate might be, he did not arrogate to himself a crown unless in the most exceptional circumstances and as a result of the election of his brother magnates.

Relying in this way on the sacredness of the royal family, the Capetians moved cautiously for a time, securing at first the 'election' of the heir during the lifetime of the reigning monarch; building up their alleged Carolingian connexions and encouraging the myth of Charles the Great in order to reflect glory on his successors as rulers of 'la douce France'; allying themselves firmly with the Church in order to secure a makeweight against the centrifugal forces of feudalism, and also because of the part played by the clergy in the coronation service. The magnates who chose one of their number as king when they elected Eudes in 888 and Hugh Capet a century later were not only demonstrating their acceptance of the need for monarchy: they were getting rid of distasteful memories of strong Carolingian rule. Yet the Capetian kings were in the long run to govern France as Charles the Great had never done, and they were partly to do it in a way which the magnates who had been responsible for their original election could have least expected—by feudal control.

In Germany monarchy had a more auspicious beginning than in France. The magnates were less numerous and less wealthy. The threat of invasion, which operated as a unifying force in France up to the settlement of the Norsemen in Normandy in 911, lasted much longer in Germany, where the Magyars were finally defeated in the battle of Lechfeld in 955 but were not converted to Christianity until 1000. But there were more potent reasons even than these. The class of free peasantry was larger in Germany than it was south of the Rhine and, as Germany had been brought under monarchical rule by Carolingian advance, the tradition of obedience established by the Carolingians remained relatively effective. Hence it was that as early as 919 the dukes threw off the rule of the old dynasty of *rois fainéants* and elected the duke of Saxony as their king. Henry I the Fowler (*d.* 936), like Hugh Capet later, founded a long-lived dynasty. It reigned unbroken till 1024. Even then the Salian dynasty which followed was closely related to the preceding Saxon kings, just as the Hohenstauffen kings were to the Salians, whom they followed in 1138. True, the succession of 'indirect' heirs in Germany gave more reality to 'election' there than it was to have in France, and occasions occurred when a very genuine election elevated to the throne a prince who was in no sense in the line of succession. Yet these acts (like the election of Lothar II in 1125) were regarded at the time as rebellious, and it is fair to say that the hereditary principle was accepted in Germany to the end of the Hohenstauffen dynasty in 1254.

In the tenth and eleventh centuries the German king was infinitely more powerful than any other monarch in the West. Master of homogeneous territories, encouraging an expansive movement of German chivalry into the Wendish lands on the Baltic and the Slav lands to the east, the king could create marcher lordships for his followers and ensure their allegiance. In the German Church, whose bishops and abbots he nominated and whose lands supplied him with military forces which could not be turned to private dynasticism, the kings had an instrument of government which they exploited to the full. To the south they interfered successfully in the troubled field of Italian politics and re-established the control which Charles the Great had acquired in the north of the peninsula. Such power did not need to be built up gradually. The German king was, certainly, the supreme feudal lord of his territories, though there were far more allodial lands in Germany than in France, but his power was essentially not feudal at this stage. He ruled for the effective reason that he was powerful and an acceptance of public authority was still native to his German subjects. The possession of *de facto* authority of a similar sort had been the background for the dramatic coronation of Charlemagne as emperor in 800. Small wonder that his German successor Otto I, who had defeated all ducal resistance in Germany, and had been victorious over the Hungarians in 955, intervened in Italy in 961 and was crowned emperor in Rome in 962. This action was more important in its way than Charlemagne's had been. For the Saxon emperors and their successors took seriously the union thus effected between the *regnum Italicum* and their

German territories and were prepared to maintain it by every possible means.

From 962 onwards German kings were, actually or potentially, emperors of the West. Doubtless the title was an added prop to their power in Germany, but northern Italy was (as we shall see) an area where town life revived more quickly than elsewhere in Europe and was consequently a rich possession. Besides, there was another connexion between the emperor and Italy—the Church. Charles the Great's visit to Rome in 800 had been to defend the reigning pope. In 961 Otto had answered a call from Pope John XII, a magnate who had acquired the papacy in order to dominate the other magnates of central Italy; after his coronation Otto deposed John. In Germany the king was undisputed master of the Church, responsible to God for its moral well-being and often interested, if only for selfish reasons, in securing for it uncorrupt and able officers. Was it not even more the emperor's task to ensure a decent papacy? At any rate it was through the emperors that the papacy was reformed. Otto III made a beginning in this direction, but the decisive step was taken in the reign of Henry III (*d.* 1056). In 1046 the papacy was the disputed possession of three unworthy 'popes'; they were swept away by the emperor and replaced by a German prelate; before his death Henry had successively nominated three further German reformers to the throne of St. Peter. Later emperors were to suffer for this. The unquestioned power of kings over clergy was one thing: the reformed papacy was to ask whether this power was justified.

The need for Church reform was evident enough

before the eleventh century. The clergy aspired to greater holiness than ordinary men and, as an aid to the single-minded service of God, all clergy, secular as well as regular, professed celibacy. Yet many priests had mistresses and sometimes openly married, founding families where son followed father as priest, in much the same way as son followed father on the servile tenements of the manor or in the noble feofs of the knightly class. Concubinage and open marriage seem to have been most common during the tenth and eleventh centuries in Italy and Germany, though priests with regular or irregular consorts were found in every part of western Christendom, while perhaps the worst examples of father being followed by son in a Church office come from the Breton dioceses of Quimper and Nantes, where the bishoprics themselves were thus transmitted. Surrounded by such laxity in the secular clergy it is hardly odd that many monasteries lapsed from the rigour of the Benedictine rule and permitted their inmates to live in great comfort even when not in more flagrant sin.

The higher appointments in the Church were, in addition, of great social prestige. A bishop or an abbot was often a powerful lord. This led to two dangers. On the one hand a prelate might spend all his time wrangling and fighting for his rights as a lay baron; we have noticed above (p. 64) some examples of bishops who were military officers in virtue of their position as vassals; many more were soldiers by inclination rather than duty and very few were like the tenth-century Bishop Lambert of Milan who in the end repented bitterly of his horrible crimes and oppressions. On the other hand higher clerical appointments could be turned to profit by their incumbents and ambitious clerics were prepared to cringe to powerful men, to flatter them, to bribe them outright, in order to secure promotion. Plenty of examples of the purchase of high office could be adduced: many nobles were like the count of Toulouse and another southern magnate who combined in 1016 to charge 100,000 shillings (*solidi*) as the price of nominating to the archbishopric of Narbonne; many kings were like the Emperor Conrad II who in 1025 appointed bishops to Liége and Basle in return for substantial money payments. The clergy who secured advancement in this way regarded the bribe as an investment. 'I get some gold for ordaining a priest', Gerbert of Aurillac (Pope Sylvester II, *d.* 1008), makes a corrupt bishop say, 'I make a man deacon and I am paid silver; for other orders, for blessing abbeys and churches, I am sure of making a profit, so that the cash I've spent is back again in my treasury.' Even the courtiers whom princes sometimes chose on grounds of political efficiency could not be relied upon to take the religious side of their office seriously, and not a few must have echoed the remark reported to have been made by the wicked Manasses, who possessed himself of the archbishopric of Rheims in 1069: he complained that the office would have been 'enjoyable if it had not been incumbent on its holder to say masses'. Yet warrior bishops or courtly abbots also intensified the disorders among the lower clergy, for as we have seen the bishop was responsible for the secular priests in his diocese and often for the monks as well. A campaign against sexual incontinence and simony (the sin of Simon Magus, bribery for promotion) was needed. How was it to be organized? Cluny was one approach to the problem (above, p. 66), a revived Benedictine rule, rigidly applied through a centralizing system which made monks their own masters, lifting them out of episcopal control. Many other monasteries, quite apart from Cluny, had sought from the pope, and obtained, immunity from visitation by the 'ordinary' (i.e. the local bishop), becoming directly responsible to the papacy. To the advantages of this (and they were not always very obvious) Cluny added the strong hand of the abbot of the mother-house. Yet Cluny only reformed monks and was, in a sense, aiming to dissociate monks from the tensions and trials which beset the secular clergy. If and when more general reform came, the multitude of Cluniac houses now spreading all over Europe could provide a pool of clergy for promotion to high office. But by itself Cluniac reform did little for the Church as a whole.

Another approach to the problem lay in the many attempts which were made by individual reforming bishops. In Italy there were outstanding bishops like Atto of Vercelli (*d*. 964) and Rathier (*d*. 968) at Verona; in Germany we may mention Wolfgang at Ratisbon (*d*. 994), and his two successors in the same see, Bernard (*d*. 1022) and Gothard (*d*. 1039); while in France the most notable were Gérard at Toul (*d*. 994) and Fulbert at Chartres (*d*. 1029). These men were indefatigable in visiting their dioceses, in checking abuse, in raising the very low standard of clerical literacy and in fighting for an incorrupt and chaste clergy. Yet a good bishop might be followed by a bad one—some rich man's son or a relation of the prince—and all the good work might be undone. The case of the archbishopric of Sens illustrates this point. In 958 the see was occupied by the unscrupulous soldier Archembaud and for nine years he polluted it with every kind of excess. Anastasius, who followed him (967–977) was quite the reverse, a pious and devout man who initiated reform in his province; this was continued by the next holder of the office, Seguin (977–999) another saintly figure, and by his successor Liétry (999–1032): 'a veritable renaissance took place in the diocese'. But in 1032 Gelduin bought the office, was forcibly installed by the French King Henry I, and in a few months ruined the reformation of the preceding seventy years: he was 'another Archembaud'. Unless a continuous succession of good bishops could be ensured reform would always be fitful and liable to lapse. Unless the Church organized itself as a unity for reform and accomplished a general reformation, partial and piecemeal amelioration would be doomed to failure.

There was never any doubt who should take the lead in such a general programme of reformation—the pope. It would be tedious and disagreeable to rehearse the lives of the unworthy successors of St. Peter in the ninth and tenth centuries. Frequently the private possession of a Roman magnate, often disputed between several claimants, regularly held by immature or vicious men, the papal office was filled by election, as in Church law it should have been, by the clergy and people of Rome. There was no local king to appoint the pope, though emperors occasionally did so, as we have seen. Yet, despite the low quality of its occupants, St. Peter's see steadily acquired more prestige and importance as time went on. We have already had occasion to notice the twin bases of this: appeals for guidance on matters of Church administration and law from the clergy in the provinces to the senior bishop in the West; and the possession by the popes of a vast territory in the centre of Italy.

The power of the pope as an arbiter in matters of Church organization and discipline was reflected in the growing coherence of Canon law: the law of the Church. This was based on the vast mass of specific decisions which popes had made from time to time (decretals) and which were collected as precedents for future action by the clerks in the papal *curia*. It was also based on a more theoretical approach, by the desire to provide precedents where none existed, by a positive and aggressive legal policy. This may be seen in the False Decretals, a collection of spurious papal decisions of allegedly early date which began to circulate in the ninth century. This mass of accepted precedent, genuine and invented, was reduced to a more systematic form by the clerical jurist Gratian in the twelfth century, but long before that clerical lawyers had been prepared to argue more forcibly than popes the authority of their master as head of the Church: the False Decretals, indeed, went further and argued the complete independence of the hierarchy of the Church from any lay control. Such a claim was supported by an even more celebrated document, the Donation of Constantine. This was fabricated rather earlier than the False Decretals. In the form of an imperial rescript, it purported to transfer rights over the western Empire to the popes of Rome.

As far as practical power was concerned the popes of the tenth and eleventh centuries were far from living up to pretensions such as these. Yet the resources for practical power lay ready to hand. The endowments of the Roman church were, like those of all others, in land; and they were very large. The pope had, moreover, an interest in converting landed power into financial power. The lands of the papacy were regarded primarily as a source of taxation. To this revenue (which depended on the efficiency of the pope and his deputies) must be added the money paid by 'exempt' monasteries all over western Christendom (above, p. 93), and the more erratic tribute which was occasionally paid by the perimeter princes of the north and west, Peter's Pence. Besides these sources of income, similar in kind, though larger than the feudal revenue (*regalia*) of any bishopric, there were the sums collected in the churches of Rome from the many visitors and pilgrims; these alms and oblations were called the 'spiritual income' (*spiritualia*) of a church. Though fluctuating, this was large in the principal churches of Rome, being shared between the pope and the clergy of the church where it had been collected. These were the main sources of papal income in the tenth century. It will be evident that the see of St. Peter was a prize much coveted by the turbulent magnates of central Italy and that it could, in the hands of a determined man, be made into a temporal power of considerable weight.

In the middle of the eleventh century, as we have noted, the Emperor Henry III deposed some corrupt popes and placed in the papal chair a series of high-minded prelates, resolved that the papacy must play its part in stamping out the sins of clerical incontinence and simony. As the ultimate interpreter of Canon law the popes had a key position: however sensual priests and monks may have been, the law on celibacy had never wavered; equally it was laid down that prelates must be elected by clergy and people, not appointed by great princes. All were agreed that the bishops were the key men in making good the moral reformation of the clergy. Accordingly it was obvious that the papacy must play its part by securing an unfettered and righteous episcopate. This position the popes who followed Henry III's first nominee, Clement II (*d.* 1047), gradually found themselves taking up. Leo IX (*d.* 1054) was an indefatigable worker, visiting France and Germany and in the many synods of bishops over which he presided infecting the prelates with his zeal and earnestness for reform. Wherever possible prelates who had secured their promotion through bribery were deposed and immoral monks and priests were punished, while the need for canonical election was stressed. The first stage in this process of papal leadership of reform came when, in the pontificate of Nicholas II (*d.* 1061), it was ruled that only the chief clergy of Rome had the power to elect a pope, such an election not necessarily taking place in Rome. This step was logical enough. How could the pope urge canonical election for lesser prelates if he owed his own appointment to an imperial nomination? One consequence of the decree was to give more concrete form to the entourage of the pope. The 'cardinal' clergy emerge more and more as a distinct corporation, rising in prestige with the papacy, and a source, moreover, of future popes, for the cardinals who met in 'conclave' on the death of a pope more often than not chose one of themselves as his successor. The emperor's advisers and local supporters in Italy (Henry IV was a child when he succeeded his father in 1056) viewed these developments with hostility and maintained an anti-pope for a time. But papal legates toured France and Germany, and Alexander II (d. 1073), elected under the new provisions, was universally accepted as true pope.

Matters came to a head when Cardinal Hildebrand was elected pope as Gregory VII in 1073. Hildebrand, an Italian peasant by origin and a monk by early training, had for long been an influence behind the scenes. He was an opinionated and devoted supporter of papal leadership in reform and carried on the moral reformation of the clergy with even greater reliance than his predecessors on the high claims of the papacy as the repository of earthly power in the Christian community. Henry IV was faced by civil war in Germany and was not able to interfere. In 1075 Gregory took the critical step of forbidding lay investiture, whereby princes had given prelates the symbol of their spiritual authority at the time of appointment. Thus began the so-called 'investiture contest'.

The facts of the conflict may be briefly told. The issue of Gregory's prohibitions had been determined by a disputed election to the archbishopric of Milan, where the contenders were a canonically elected reformer and an imperial nominee. The emperor relied on the Italian bishops to govern Italy as he did on the German bishops at home and he was not prepared to allow Gregory's fiat to go unchallenged. Gregory threatened to depose Henry: Henry promptly declared that Gregory was not true pope. In the spring of 1076 Gregory excommunicated the emperor and invited the imperial vassals to desert their master. Henry had only just finished with one rebellion; the pope's action was calculated to make civil war endemic; the emperor resolved to capitulate at once and hurried over the Alps at Christmas, 1076. Gregory was sheltering in the fortress of Canossa when the emperor came before him as a penitent, barefoot in the snow. Gregory hesitated: but his religion was one of forgiveness and, though he must have realized what consequences his action would have, he readmitted Henry into the bosom of the Church. It was later useless for the pope to seek to arbitrate between Henry and his rebellious subjects in Germany. Henry slowly put down rebellion, although excommunicated afresh in 1080, and the very magnitude of Gregory's demand to be the superior of any emperor lost him support in Germany. Soon Henry could invade Italy, and it was as an exile among the brigand Norman nobles in the south of the peninsula that Gregory died in 1085. Subsequent popes and emperors continued the struggle with less determination until, in the concordat made at Worms in 1122, a sensible compromise was arrived at, which (broadly speaking) preserved the structure of canonical election while allowing the emperor a right of veto; similar solutions were arrived at in all the main countries of Christendom.

In a sense the result of the 'investiture contest' was a foregone conclusion. How could any priest dispute the real power of the lay prince? True, the terrors of excommunication were sincerely felt, and the papacy had already tried to enlist widespread lay support for reform by forbidding laymen to hear Mass celebrated by married priests. But canonical investiture, though seen by the pope as a necessary stage in moral reformation, was rather different; and to remove a lord's vassals by excommunication was to appeal to their most sordid lust for land and might end in universal anarchy. It was generally felt that the Church had gone too far, and the issue of investiture was not raised again in a sharp form even by later popes with a greater sense of theocratic power than Gregory VII. Even more significant, proprietary rights over parish churches remained untouched, so that the lay patron of a living could continue, as before, to nominate to the cure of souls.

The consequences of the debate between pope and emperor between 1075 and 1122 were vaster than the stalemate on investiture would suggest. They may be seen on the one hand in the rapid rise of papal pretensions and the fillip given to political speculation, and on the other in the deterioration which began in the government of the Empire. This last question will occupy us in the next chapter and we will conclude this by discussing the growth of papal claims to earthly power because it led to the first abstract formulation of political ideals in the Christian society of the West.

The Christian speculation which was jerked into rapid movement after 1075 had roots in the past. From the Greeks (by way of the Fathers and Boethius) had come some Stoic notions which attributed government and the power of men over men to human corruption. Such a doctrine fitted in well with the Christian view of the Fall. Government was part of God's machinery for a corrupt and sinful mankind. With this view of the State, bondage, and earthly punishments most later writers agreed, and the notion gradually grew up that, in this abstract sense, there were several sorts of 'law'—the divine or natural law which was God's plan at work in the world and in man, and part of which was 'revealed' in the Scriptures; the *jus gentium* or law of nations was really part of this, a sort of corpus of universally accepted rights and wrongs; particular local laws enforced by positive sanctions were finally necessary according to local circumstance. Civil power was thus a part of the divine arrangement as a result of Adam's fall from grace: 'render unto Caesar the things that are Caesar's'. The early Christians had indeed interpreted this commandment literally and had sought to turn their backs on the Terrestrial City, placing all their hopes on the City of God. But, from Constantine onwards, the Church and the civil community were theoretically one and in the centuries which followed the identification grew more effective. All men were baptized into the world. Kings, emperors, and great men might be all-powerful over clergy and laity, yet they were children of God and could call a priest their father.

This compromise, real power in the hands of the lay prince who yet submitted to the spiritual guidance of the clergy, was for long not upset, though the Donation of Constantine and the False Decretals showed that it was possible for the successor of St. Peter to urge his rights as moral custodian of the West. The change came not from the ambitions of lay princes, but from a reforming papacy. To secure his control over the Church Gregory VII was prepared, albeit unwillingly, to damn all political power as a product of sin and claim what amounted to a power to remove princes at will if in his view they offended against the teaching of the Church. This authority in secular matters was based on spiritual foundations. Later popes made this more explicit still. A century after Gregory VII, Innocent III (*d.* 1216) was placed in circumstances which enabled him to arrogate to the papacy the right of determining on what terms England and France should make peace with one another; besides this, he humbled Philip II Augustus of France over an unlawful divorce (1198) and John of England over a disputed election to the archbishopric of Canterbury, John finally becoming a 'vassal' of the pope (1213). These autocratic gestures show how far papal interference in lay affairs had left the noble aim of purifying the clergy, the narrow issue of investiture, and the restricted area of the Empire; though events enabled Innocent III to make good his claims as an arbiter in imperial affairs too, as we shall note later. Such interventions were, of course, not made without an ethical purpose: and the doctrine that the pope was superior to all lay rulers whom he could control directly if he chose, which became official in the pontificate of Innocent IV (*d.* 1254), was tempered by the understanding that the pope would act only in cases of sin. But it was clear that only the pope could judge what was sin and from the position reached by the early thirteenth century it was but a short step to the unequivocal claim of Boniface VIII (*d.* 1303) that 'it was necessary for salvation that all men should be subject to the Roman pope'. This assertion is really the start of a fresh period of political speculation and we shall return to it later (below,

p. 176). Here we may note that it would probably not have been made so early had not the milder statements of earlier popes provoked a vigorous reply and had not the papacy itself acquired in the twelfth and thirteenth centuries concrete economic and political advantages which made its programme more than a piece of bombast.

Gregory VII and his successors certainly set the pace in the argument over investiture and the deeper problems of simony and incontinence. Their imperial opponents were hampered by certain assumptions which they shared with their opponents, that in the cosmic hierarchy (above, p. 76), a priest was nearer God than a layman, that the Donation of Constantine was genuine and that, by crowning Charlemagne, Leo III conferred on his successors some say in the creation of all emperors. The imperial propagandists were almost all clergymen and consequently moved cautiously, stressing those texts in the Bible which showed established authority as of divine origin, and those ceremonies and attributes of monarchy which were priest-like. The imperialists thus stuck to the Gelasian equality of the 'spiritual sword' and the 'temporal sword' (above, p. 27). But Frederick Barbarossa (d. 1190) and Frederick II (d. 1250) were mighty political forces in the twelfth and thirteenth centuries. Their answer, like the answer given by a French bureaucrat to Boniface VIII, was, in effect: 'You may have the right, we have the power.'

The power of the pope in the time of Boniface VIII had in fact declined from the height it had reached under Innocent III. Administratively the organs of the papal court or *curia* continued to develop: the chancery with its elaborate offices for sending out papal bulls (so called from the lead *bulla* or seal appended to the document) in answer to the requests and inquiries of the faithful; the *camera apostolica* or treasury department, which handled the income from subsidies, taxation, indulgences, and the hundred and one other sources of revenue which now accrued to the headquarters of the Church; and the legal administration, from the pope with his cardinals in consistory, the supreme court of the hierarchy, down to the deputies of the Apostolic Penitentiary, whose job it was to release individuals who had been anathematized for offences which were reserved to the pope for absolution. All this machinery was, in fact, to reach its highest point of development under the fourteenth-century popes who followed Boniface VIII (below, p. 177), but Innocent III's real power was greater than that of any later pope. We have seen some of the occasions on which he intervened forcefully in the affairs of secular princes, and such examples could have been multiplied.

Innocent also ruled the Church with a strong hand. Bishops were compelled to make periodical visits to Rome and did not regard themselves as having been properly appointed without papal approval. Himself a lawyer, Innocent's pontificate saw a further increase in appeals to Rome. Above all, this shrewd and pertinacious man saw the immense power which lay to his hand in two contemporary movements which he did his best to harness to the papal cause: the universities (above, p. 74) and the friars (below, p. 210). At almost the end of his pontificate he held a General Council (known as the Fourth Lateran Council) in which he and the assembled prelates

LAW AND GOVERNMENT 105

legislated over the whole field of Christian discipline, and, in particular, against the heretics who, from this period onwards are a permanent feature of the Church in the West (below, p. 208.) Against them the Fourth Lateran Council thundered the fiercest penalties and invoked lay support: a temporal lord who refused to purge his land of heretics was to be excommunicated and to forfeit the fealty of his vassals; and a war against heretics was to earn indulgences for the combatants previously extended only to crusaders. Other noteworthy canons of the council were those which called for provincial councils and episcopal synods every year; condemned the judicial ordeal as earlier councils had condemned the judicial duel (above, p. 71); and laid down that 'every Christian of either sex, after reaching years of discretion, shall faithfully confess all his sins, at least once a year, privately to his own priest'. Yet Innocent's Lateran Council also shows that the assembled clergy were essentially rubber-stamping policy worked out in the *curia*. For all practical purposes Innocent III was superior in practice even over a General Council of the whole Church, let alone over the emperor and other lay princes, as he claimed to be.

Innocent III (and certain of his immediate successors, like Innocent IV) had the ability to make papal theocracy a conceivable form for Christian society. We must remember that in the first half of the thirteenth century the area recognizing the Roman pontiff was almost coterminous with Christendom: the Fourth Crusade (below, p. 131) had brought the eastern Empire (under a Latin patriarch of Constantinople) under the papal wing. Such a papal theocracy was, in a sense, a mere variation on the totalitarian régime which had existed in the Greek Empire before the Fourth Crusade. There the emperor, Equal of the Apostles (to quote one of his titles), was head of both Church and secular government. Could not the pope have occupied a similar position in the West? It was, from Gregory VII onwards, the programme of the papacy to do just that.

The attempt was more than merely political, more even than a worthy attempt to reform the Church and secure a truly Christian laity. It reflected a profound consciousness that, in the last resort, the peoples dwelling under the decentralized powers of feudal society were members of Christendom. The values of feof and manor no doubt had a complete stranglehold on the partial efforts of the devout to emancipate the clergy, let alone the whole of society, from mundane paths. But the element binding together the serf and his lord, the lords and peasants of one kingdom and those of all other areas, was their common religion. The Christian could not be a slave, and, as we have seen, though the condition of many peasants was desperate, they had clearly defined and respected rights. To enter into this Christian society a man was baptized; the font conferred an entry into a vast corporation contrasted by its members with the benighted pagan races to whom light was as yet denied. It was this acceptance of corporate Christianity which gave the penalty of excommunication its singular efficacy. To fall under anathema meant that a man was automatically deprived of his membership of the Church in its widest aspect. He was not only denied the consolations of religion and the services of a priest. He was an outlaw and an outcast, and all other Christians had to shun him. He had (to quote the Roman *ordo excommunicandi*) betrayed his baptismal promise and was cut off from the sacrament of communion, the society of all Christians, the threshold of the Church in heaven and on earth, and was damned with the Devil and the fallen angels. From the eleventh century this terrible punishment was commonly laid not only on individuals but on whole communities— on recalcitrant churches, towns, kingdoms. This cutting off a territory from the community of the faithful (interdict) was to lead in the end to a general disregard of excommunication, yet its original efficacy is the best evidence possible for the concrete sense of a *societas omnium Christianorum*, a 'corporation of all the faithful'. There is some truth in the paradox that the only 'State' in the Middle Ages, the only universal authority remotely comparable to the sovereign bodies of later ages, was the Church.

Such an identification of 'Church' and 'State' cannot but appear today as a monstrous aberration. At the time of which we are writing, the eleventh and twelfth centuries, the very terms themselves had hardly been adumbrated and were certainly not antithetical. Any imperialist would readily have admitted that 'Church' and 'State' were one: his argument would have been that the emperor was God's vice-regent, the custodian of Christendom. It was, however, to be the later resistance to 'caesaropapism', papal theocracy, which gradually led men to define a *respublica*, a *civitas*, a 'State' in opposition to the 'Church'. A necessary preliminary to this development was the emergence of strong principates which were not compromised (as the Empire was bound to be) by an ambivalent relationship with the papacy. The origins of such independent powers will be one of the topics occupying our attention in the following chapter.

CHAPTER V

BARONS, BISHOPS, AND KINGS

Public affairs prior to the thirteenth century narrowly localized; the magnates' aim: to equate land with government; the problems of a baron; the enlargement of territorial lordship; warfare and religion, the First Crusade; German expansion; kings and the feudality; the closing of an epoch.

WE have just considered some important features of the period from 800 to about 1250: customary law, the survival of monarchy, the great power acquired by kings of Germany, the questions of Church reform and papal claims to determine the political as well as the spiritual development of Christendom. Yet in a sense such matters as the strife between popes and emperors were peripheral at the time. It cannot be too strongly urged that, however illogical it may sound, the general history of Europe before the late thirteenth century is essentially *local* history. The public affairs which troubled the vast majority of men were, geographically speaking, narrowly circumscribed. Tyranny (as the monkish historians called the acts of a ruler they disliked, king or duke or simple knight) and disorder, peace and *bonne policie*, extended usually no farther afield than the area of a modern county or *département*. Thus to give exclusive attention to the germinating seeds of monarchy is to falsify the contemporary scene. Even in precocious Germany and England, the king was a distant figure unless one lived directly on his personal lands, the royal domain. The politics of the village were dominated by the local lord, and his activities were more often than not entangled in the schemes of magnates little grander than himself. One has only to study a chronicle of the eleventh or twelfth century to find oneself driven to the footnotes for identifications of obscure barons living in castles that have long since crumbled into anonymity. The hierarchies of feudal society and of Church organization which we have been discussing are only meaningful if we remember that government—the actual exercise of power by some men over others—was at the time utterly decentralized.

The future definition of ideals of government doubtless owed much to the investiture contest and subsequent propaganda conflicts between pope and emperor. For the ruling class of the period, for the 'powers that be' of St. Paul, political theory was simpler and can be summarized in one word: land. How to get more land, how to keep the land one already had, how to secure that one's status and authority should be related to one's landed resources, these were the ambitions of the baronage. Nor, as we have seen, were kings at first much different, though they had a tradition which put them apart from ordinary land-holders and which was to lead them to programmes scarcely compatible with a purely feudal form of power.

What were the threats to the baron's power over his lands? In the first place, other land-hungry magnates like himself. Given an opportunity, some loophole in local custom, some minor infringement of codes of tenure, some censure of the Church which led a magnate to be excommunicated and so temporarily removed from civilized society, and his lord and his neighbours might attack, occupy, and possess themselves of his lands by *force majeure*. In any case the right to make war was generally accepted as part of the rights of lordship and was, indeed, a legitimate alternative to legal processes for the settlement of disputes among men of the knightly class (above, p. 49). Except in England, where private war was effectively prohibited by the Crown, armed conflicts of magnates and their allies and retainers occurred too frequently for examples to be given here. From the ninth to the twelfth centuries all over continental Europe barons regularly chose to act *per guerram* rather than *per placitum*, by the sword rather than the law-court. Thereafter kings gradually reduced the frequency of private war, though often they enlisted the acquisitiveness of the chivalry in order to secure territorial expansion, as in the furious 'crusade' against the heretic French nobles in the south of France during the first quarter of the thirteenth century. Besides destroying the Albigensian heretics (below, p. 208) and a precocious vernacular culture of great value, the rapacious northern knights who volunteered for the attack on the count of Toulouse and other nobles of the area obtained the feofs of the dispossessed and slaughtered southern baronage. The result was that kings of France increased their authority in the Midi, but they did not manage to stamp out private war until the end of the fifteenth century.

In the second place, a magnate was threatened by

the more or less legitimate demands of his own sons. Primogeniture was by no means universal, though it was common in northern France, and when a magnate's lands were evenly divided among his heirs there was a marked reduction in the value of each portion.[1] This was a real problem, for barons were often prolific parents, frequently being blessed with four or five warrior sons. Some sons could go into the Church and might, with strong parental support, reach a fat abbacy or bishopric; some might, by a timely marriage, acquire an heiress and ultimately her lands and title. These compensations were naturally more readily available to the great magnates than to the lesser men. A study of the domestic history of any great house in the tenth, eleventh, and twelfth centuries—the counts of Vermandois, the dukes and counts of Burgundy, the counts of Flanders, to name only a few French examples—reveals the process at work.

Consider the house of Blois. In the mid-tenth century Thibaut I's children included, besides his successor Eudes I, Archbishop Hugh of Bourges, Emma who married a duke of Aquitaine, Hildegarde who married a Montmorenci lord of Bray. Eudes I (*d.* 995) was succeeded in turn by Thibaut II and Eudes II, while another son became bishop of Beauvais. Eudes II (*d.* 1037), who had inherited the county of Champagne in 1019, left his son Stephen as count of Champagne and Brie, and his other son Thibaut III as count of Blois, Tours, and Chartres.

[1] Absolute primogeniture on the English model is seldom found on the Continent where, even if priority is accorded to the eldest son, the other sons were usually given lesser feofs out of the paternal inheritance, at any rate when this was composed of a complex of feofs.

The Champagne inheritance was reacquired brutally by Thibaut on his brother's death in 1048; Stephen's son Eudes, however, secured a wealthy English heiress in the countess of Aumâle. Thibaut, who died about 1090, could thus make one son count of Champagne and another count of Blois; a third became bishop of Chalons-sur-Marne. Count Hugh of Champagne had only one son (whom he refused to recognize and who was ultimately provided for by King Louis VI) and finally became a Knight Templar. But the progeny of Count Stephen of Blois, who was alleged to possess as many castles as there were days in the year, had a glorious future. Stephen, who died in Palestine in 1102, had married the daughter of King William I of England: of the four sons who lived to mature years, one married a French heiress, one followed in the county of Champagne, one became bishop of Winchester, and one, Stephen, king of England (*d.* 1154); each of the four daughters married a count. Thibaut IV, who succeeded Stephen in 1102, had offspring who were equally successful. Of his four sons, three divided the patrimony and one became successively bishop of Chartres, archbishop first of Sens and later of Rheims, and cardinal. Of his six daughters, only one entered a nunnery, two married counts, two married dukes, and one a king of France, Louis VII.

But this was a great house, with vast territorial possessions. What of the lesser men? Is it surprising that the twelve sons of an eleventh-century Norman gentleman, Tancred de Hauteville (five by his first wife, seven by his second) should have been doughty warriors? Only two of them stayed with their father, the other ten sought their fortune elsewhere (below, p. 123). For many younger sons the future was bleak unless war opened the way to booty and fresh land. 'It is a great shame and a *great loss*', writes a French poet about the year 1200, 'for a youth to pass his early manhood without enterprise [*sans esploit*], for it is at this age that one must acquire enough worldly wealth to last the rest of one's life.' The temptation to defraud one's own relatives was great, and many families must have been like those counts of Soissons of whom Guibert of Nogent writes that 'there was mutual hatred between the generations'. One contemporary, indeed, puts into the mouth of Pope Urban at Clermont (1095, below, p. 126) the explicit statement that there was not enough land in the West; 'this land you inhabit ... is overfilled by your numbers: it does not abound in wealth; it supplies scarcely enough food for those who farm it; hence it is that you fight and devour each other, that you wage wars and often perish by mutual blows'.

A third embarrassment for the baron lay in the tendency for his own unfree servants to arrogate to themselves the offices he had conferred on them and for his vassals to contract feudal relations of a perfectly legitimate kind with his enemies or potential enemies. The former may be illustrated copiously from German history, where the *ministeriales* formed, as already noted (above, p. 51), a kind of inferior knightly class. Some members of this class could reach great wealth, like the twelfth-century *ministerialis* Werner of Bolland, who 'possessed 17 castles and had 1,100 knights in his service'. Of the other type of trouble, the most august examples are the magnates who, though subject to the French king, became vassals of the English king. This double allegiance is, however, common at all levels of the feudal ladder (above, p. 50).

A further danger lay in the vague powers of the king. Obedience to the king meant that the baron opened himself to all sorts of obnoxious interferences with his legal and administrative powers. Disobedience might, if the king was powerful and the baron without friends, lead to his being stripped of all his feudal possessions, or, a punishment only less dreadful, to his castles being destroyed.

Finally, there was a gradual shift towards cash values during the twelfth century (we have noticed the commutation of military service for cash payments above, p. 53) and this was accelerated during the thirteenth. We shall have more to say of this later (p. 171), but we may note it here as the most potent factor militating against the equation, land = government, on which the baron based his ambitions and his way of life. For the time being we will ignore it and see how he succeeded in dealing with the main issue as already defined: the extension of his territorial power.

The rulers of Anjou are a famous example. The family was originally given the countship by a late ninth-century Carolingian king. For a century the counts pursued a relatively unambitious policy. In close alliance with the Church, which they endowed on many occasions, they provided their due quota of bishops from their younger sons, and the eldest son regularly followed his father in the countship. But from Geoffrey I onwards, who came into conflict with an equally acquisitive count of Poitiers and who seems to have gained a foothold in the royal court as

'Seneschal of France', a new and aggressive spirit may be seen. Fulk III, called Nerra or the Black, who succeeded in 987, was 'warlike, subtle, and up to every trick'; he made good his power in the Touraine by defeating the count of Blois; in a pitched battle he overthrew and killed his brother-in-law, the count of Rennes; he captured by a ruse and held prisoner for two years the count of Maine; he married his two daughters into noble families, twice went on pilgrimage to the Holy Land, raised many great fortresses to protect his lands, and founded many monasteries. His successor in 1040 was his son Geoffrey II, Martel (the Hammer). He had already tried out his military skill against his father, who had disapproved of his marriage to Agnes, daughter of a count of Burgundy and widow of a count of Poitiers. This violence characterized the rest of his life: he defeated and killed the count of Poitiers; captured the count of Blois and forced him to hand over Tours; he then turned his attentions to the county of Maine which he succeeded in dominating by deceit and bullying. But Geoffrey had no sons, and two of his nephews struggled to make good their claims to succeed him in 1060—Geoffrey III and Fulk IV, surnamed Le Rechin or 'the Quarreller'. The two brothers at first jointly defended their inheritance against the attacks of the duke of Aquitaine, but soon fell out between themselves and resorted to open war: by cunning the Quarreller seized his brother in 1067 and imprisoned him for the rest of his days in the great castle of Chinon. This civil war involved concessions to both the king of France and the duke of Normandy, the two most powerful neighbours of the Angevins; to compensate for this, and for four unsuccessful marriages, Fulk Le Rechin greatly increased his control over the clergy and organized an efficient administration in his reduced lands. His successor, Fulk V, resumed the tradition of acquisitiveness by occupying Maine in the name of his wife (1110) and later Alençon; he ruthlessly brought the Angevin vassals to obedience; and, on the second of two visits to the Holy Land, he was crowned King of Jerusalem in 1129, starting a fresh dynasty in this doomed province. But the Angevins had arrived at a point of grandeur and influence which made it unnecessary for them to seek kingdoms in the Orient. Geoffrey Plantagenet, who succeeded in 1129 when his father became king in the East, married Matilda, daughter of Henry I of England and widow of the German emperor, Henry V. On his father-in-law's death, Geoffrey invaded Normandy and after eight years made himself master of the duchy. Accordingly his successor had a rich inheritance: Henry was count of Anjou, count of Maine, duke of Normandy, and king of England.[1] At this point Anjou is swallowed up in the greater affairs of France and England, but not before its rulers have aptly illustrated the aggrandizement which was possible through treachery, marriage, and war.

Not all magnates succeeded in attaching to themselves royal insignia; but other parts of France, Flanders, Aquitaine and, of course, Normandy had a not dissimilar history. If the great families of Germany, the dukes of Saxony, Franconia, Swabia, and Bavaria owed their rise to non-feudal factors, the history of Lorraine and the remnants of the kingdom of Burgundy exhibit features strictly

[1] Through his wife he had Aquitaine.

similar to those we have observed as characteristic of Anjou. But these are the great and the successful magnates. What of the masses of less important knights? Here we can be less sure of fairly illustrating the typical, for only occasionally can we trace them in our sources, and then usually when they are rebels resisting a greater man or mere vassals in his train, witnessing a charter or seeking his concurrence in some grant of land to the Church. The brutal baron is well enough attested. He found the monastery in his neighbourhood too easy a prey to abstain from violence, little caring that monastic historians would secure for him a grim immortality. The feudal gallery of rogues could be amply filled from both the south and the north of France in the tenth and eleventh centuries. Some blackguards emerge with a distinct personality, like Thomas de Marle, lord of Coucy (near Laon), whose brutal aggressions are described both by Suger, abbot of Saint-Denis (below, p. 135) and by Guibert, abbot of Nogent-sous-Coucy, Thomas's querulous and observant neighbour. Such selfish brutality as was shown by 'tyrants who provoke wars, indulge themselves in pillage, persecute the poor and destroy churches' (to quote Suger), brought a reaction from the better sort of lord, who supported any concerted movement for 'peace' or 'truce' (below, p. 127) and aided the king to enforce a modicum of order.

In the preceding pages we have illustrated the dynasticism of the successful magnates, operating within existing territorial estates. There were, however, two other ways in which the knight could satisfy his need for more land. First, he could extend the valuable land inside existing areas of cultivation, 'internal colonization'; second, by going beyond the frontiers of Christendom he could secure estates from the pagans on the perimeter, a process of external expansion. The baronage employed both methods, but the second from the start was more attractive.

The only area in which internal colonization was taken up on a massive scale by the knightly class was Germany. In France and Italy all but the poorest land had lain under lordship for long and the marginal land was seldom easy or attractive even to an impecunious nobility. The establishment of new villages on the waste during the twelfth and thirteenth centuries led in these areas mainly to an enlargement of existing lordships rather than to the creation of new estates. In England, the peculiar tenurial arrangements established by the Conquest put all land ultimately under the king, discouraging knightly enterprise of this sort, and in England the king's rights over the forest were jealously guarded. But in Germany there was an allodial tradition (above, p. 52) and there was much land lying ready to be wrested from the forest. From secure bases in allodial property large numbers of German nobles extended their area of domination by absorbing freshly colonized lands which, since they had been wrested from the virgin forest, were treated as nonfeudal; and when the conglomeration of power was sufficiently great, they claimed the title of count with correspondingly wide rights. Often the pioneers in colonization were monasteries; but the magnates who became 'advocates' (above, p. 64, Ger. *Vogt*) of these new lands soon absorbed them into their own domains. The existence of large areas of forest land in the very heart of Germany, like the Black Forest, meant that these developments were not restricted only to the moving north-eastern frontier, but were found also in the west and south. It has been shown that many of the higher nobility of Swabia and Franconia, as well as in Bavaria, who come into the twelfth-century limelight as fully-fledged dynastic princelings, have their origins in the processes of internal colonization. As we shall notice shortly (p. 142), the extent of the internal colonization practised beyond the Rhine was to be reflected in the political evolution of Germany.

It was the second means of securing land, external expansion, which offered the most continuous outlet to the baronage. Western Christendom was bounded by territories under pagan rule, like Moslem Spain and the Wendish and Slav lands north and east of the narrow 'Germany' of the early Middle Ages. In the Balkans and south Italy lay the domains of the eastern emperor for whom the average knight had small regard. Many of these points of expansion lay far enough away from the main centre of baronial over-population in the north of France, but that was not so much a disadvantage as might at first appear.

The habit of pilgrimage was already endemic by the tenth century, as was to be expected in the adherents of an historical religion for whom the New Testament was not only a devotional work but also a geography lesson, almost a guide-book. The places where the Apostles had prayed and been martyred were holy ground, and their relics were piously conserved and venerated in scores of churches. In Rome itself lay the bones of St. Peter and St. Paul; at St. James of Compostella in north-western Spain was one of the most sacred shrines in Christendom; and dozens of smaller places of pilgrimage existed in nearly every province of the Church. Visits to such centres were regarded as meritorious almost in proportion to the difficulties involved in getting to them. No pilgrimage therefore had greater value than the incredibly arduous journey to Jerusalem itself. Pilgrims were, of course, not drawn exclusively from the knightly class; poor men, and especially humble clergy, shared in the movement along with rich prelates and barons; many monasteries, and especially Cluniac houses, tried to smooth the pilgrims' way. But the organization of a lengthy expedition involved wealth which was normally at the disposal only of a landed magnate and his family, or one of the great prelates.

Given this general urge to show devotion by undertaking pilgrimages and the current shortage of land, it was a short step to the Crusade, the holy war fought to defend Christianity and to achieve permanent reconquest of lands lost to the infidel. It was in Spain that a *de facto* coalescence of the two motives first occurred. Crusades of a sort took place there before the official Crusade began.

The Moslems had ultimately failed to control the whole of the Spanish peninsula and tiny Christian principalities persisted in the north—Leon, Navarre, and the March established by Charlemagne. The break-up of the united Moslem Caliphate at the end of the eighth century, when Persian replaced Arab influence in the heart of the Moslem world, left an independent Arab Caliphate of Spain, based on Cordova and controlling the adjacent coastlands of North Africa. The Moslem Caliphate of Spain (whose immense cultural importance will be mentioned later, p. 213) was, however, anything but homogeneous. The Christian population (the Mozarabs) gave little trouble, but there were extreme tensions between Berbers from Africa, settled in the mountains of the centre, and the Arabs dwelling in the richest lands of Andalusia. For lengthy periods there was civil war among the Spanish Moslem leaders and this enabled the Christian kingdoms in the north gradually to advance their boundaries. The victorious soldiers were rewarded with feofs and privileges. Some had an almost royal scope for their ambitions, like the Castilian noble, Rodrigo Diaz (the Cid, *d.* 1099) in Valencia. To landless adventurers Spain offered a continuous attraction, as the enemy was rich in booty as well as in land, while Christians could rejoice in reclaiming Christian territory and rescuing the Mozarabs from contamination. Many French knights joined in the reconquest; two Spanish royal dynasties received an infusion of Burgundian blood. The kingdom of Castile, which emerged from the western half of Leon, took the lead in this advance, which achieved the capture of Toledo in 1085. From time to time a Moslem revival held up the advance, but by the mid-thirteenth century Seville and Cordova itself had fallen and there remained only the small kingdom of Granada (in the south-east) which was to last until the end of the fifteenth century (below, p. 197). In these campaigns the kingdom of Aragon arose, based on the northern Mediterranean coast, and, on the Atlantic seaboard, the small kingdom of Portugal.

The Moslems had never managed for long to maintain a foothold on the mainland of Italy, though they had dominated Sicily. The area to the south of Rome lay on one of the pilgrim routes to the East and the land offered an excellent field for ruthless men, for it was divided between warring Lombard princes (at Capua and Benevento) and remnants of the Byzantine Empire in Apulia and Calabria. While a band of Norman pilgrims were passing through the land on their way home from Jerusalem in 1016, they were involved in the domestic feuds of the area. News of the pickings soon attracted reinforcements from Normandy. Their leaders were drawn from the large family of Tancred de Hauteville (above p. 113). Robert Guiscard (*d*. 1085) managed to dominate his brothers, and the embarrassment of the popes, engaged in the task of dissociating themselves from imperial control (above p. 99), gave the Norman dynasty an authoritative supporter: in 1080 Gregory VII was compelled to recognize Guiscard as master of almost the whole of the south of the peninsula. A younger brother of Guiscard had meanwhile conquered Sicily, and it was finally from Sicily that Roger II (*d*. 1154) united the two territories in the kingdom of Sicily. Like Moslem Spain, the new kingdom was, as we shall see (p. 213), to be of great influence in the cultural development of Europe.

From Apulia across the Adriatic lay the Balkan provinces of the Byzantine Empire, again familiar to the western pilgrim who normally travelled across Greece on his way to Constantinople and the Holy Sepulchre. These territories had been an obvious target for the acquisitive Normans in south Italy: only his death had prevented Guiscard from making a frontal attack on Byzantium.

The eastern Empire had suffered much since the

days of Justinian, when it had made a last attempt to recover its lost possessions in the West (above, p. 20). It was at first the Persians who were the main enemy, but soon the Moslem attack reached Asia Minor and the emperors were really saved, not so much by the victory of Leo III the Isaurian in 717 (above, p. 34), as by the break-up of the Caliphate. While grappling with these threats from the East more and more of the Balkan territories of the Empire slipped out of imperial control. The Bulgars, a Hun tribe, had crossed the Danube in 679 and made thereafter repeated sorties against Constantinople. In the ninth century they became Christians and formed an autonomous, if barbarous, region under rulers styling themselves tsars in emulation of the caesars at Byzantium. The latter were able from time to time to enforce their will on the Bulgarian clansmen by employing mercenary troops drawn from the Scandinavians who came through the overland river routes from the Baltic to the Black Sea. Some of these 'Varangians' were now established at Novgorod and Kiev, predecessors of the future Russians. Towards the end of the tenth century they were converted to Greek Christianity.

The Empire was wealthy in trading resources, both through the Scandinavian trade and as the terminus of some of the overland routes to Asia. This produced revenue which permitted the emperors to flaunt a magnificence to which western courts could not aspire. Enabled thus to hire soldiers, the emperors were at first not embarrassed either by the failure of Byzantine society to retain the old free peasantry in Anatolia, which had been the backbone of earlier imperial armies, or by the absence of feudal relationships on the western model. The free peasantry was indeed protected by all able emperors until the early twelfth century. Then the magnates, who had added to their power the control over many monastic lands by the exercise of protection (*charisticaria*) similar to the 'advocacy' of the West (above, p. 64), were in the late twelfth and thirteenth centuries given imperial lands in return for military service (*pronoia*). But throughout the Middle Ages taxation rather than personal service remained the backbone of Byzantine administration and with money coming into the imperial treasury, Constantinople consequently remained the most splendid city in Christendom, despite the contraction of the boundaries of the Empire. The civilization of the court, the corrupt but resourceful bureaucracy with its elaborate hierarchies, the infinitely sophisticated but obedient clergy, all maintained the outward trappings of grandeur. Emperors might exhibit Oriental weaknesses: relatively few of them died of old age. But there was obviously a tremendous resilience in a State which had weathered more or less successfully the full onslaught of the German, Slav, and Hun barbarians from the North and the Persians and Arabs from the South.

The eleventh century brought, however, two novel dangers; the restless aggression of the Normans in southern Italy, and the expansion of the Seljuk Turks. The Seljuks had originally been mercenaries of the Arab Caliphate from whom they acquired the religion of Islam and a taste for power. By 1070 they had succeeded in overrunning Persia, Syria, and the Holy Land; in the following year their Sultan Alp Arslan defeated a Byzantine army at Manzikert and soon almost the whole of Anatolia was occupied by the Turks. This event was to have important consequences. First, it convinced the Byzantines that they must enlist much larger mercenary forces in their defence. Second, the tolerance showed by earlier Moslem rulers of Syria and Palestine, from the Abbasids to the Fatimids, was replaced by a harsher persecution calculated to stir up resistance among the Christians in these areas, both those nominally in communion with Constantinople and the numerous independent churches produced by schisms in the past. And third, the access of pilgrims to the Holy Land was barred. From these causes came the First Crusade: the Empire needed men, western knights needed land, and western Christians had been educated to feel that the accessibility of the Holy Places was essential to religion. These were motives which were not always compatible with one another.

The first man to be disillusioned was the Emperor Alexius I Comnenus (d. 1118), who formally appealed, through Pope Urban II (d. 1099) for Christian volunteers. At the Council of Clermont (November, 1095) Urban called on 'rich and poor' to embark on a campaign to rescue the faithful in the East. The result was not what Urban had expected nor what Alexius desired. In place of a scattered response by individual knights, the chivalry of western Christendom answered the appeal in armies, including contingents of the very Norman magnates whom Alexius knew to be deceitful and aggressive. Nor was the response confined only to the well-to-do who could adequately finance a distant military expedition: many humble men were inflamed by popular preaching of the Crusade. Was not Urban himself at

Clermont reported to have said that 'here they were poor and unhappy, there they would be joyful and prosperous and true friends of God'? Alexius may, indeed, have been doubtful about the attitude of the papacy itself, for since 1054 the latent differences between the Orthodox Christian Church of the East and the Roman Church (above, p. 25) had finally hardened into open schism. But Urban was a charitable man and not sorry either that the papacy, in the midst of its first bitter quarrel with the Roman emperor of the West, should lead a movement which would make an ally of the Roman emperor of the East.

Nor can the pope have been blind to the advantage accruing to western society if the warlike energies of the lesser baronage were deflected to the East. For a century prior to the Council of Clermont sporadic attempts had been made to limit the effects of private warfare. The first 'Peace of God' was proclaimed by the clergy of the south of France at the Council of Charroux in 989 and soon local nobles were persuaded to swear an oath which precluded them from attacking the poor, women, and unarmed clergy. Early in the eleventh century the 'Peace' was extended into an even more ambitious form, the 'Truce of God', which laid down certain times of the year when warfare was forbidden—Sundays, holydays, Lent. At the Council of Narbonne in 1054 the two approaches were combined and excommunication was laid down as the penalty for any transgressor. These developments (inspired, it must be stressed, by religious not by political motives) had been made under the impulse of the Church. It was appropriate that, in so far as the Crusade had a leader at all, it was the papal legate appointed by Urban, Adhemar, bishop of Le Puy.

The peace movement of the early eleventh century was, of course, largely ineffective, but even without it the lesser magnates had every inducement to respond to an invitation which appealed to their sense of piety as well as to their desire for land and booty. It is, in fact, significant that on this occasion the Cross was taken by not a single king and by few of the really successful nobles of the period. The greater men who went with crowds of their retainers were barons whose future at home was dim. Hugh of Vermandois was a younger brother of the king of France. Godfrey of Bouillon, another second son, had the duchy of Lower Lorraine, but not as a hereditary feof, and he was in danger of losing it for inefficiency. Bohemond of Taranto, a son of Guiscard, had been forced to fight his uncle Roger of Sicily for the Apulian duchy and could never hope to secure it all. These men were surrounded by followers anxious to promote territorial success for their lords, since they might share in it by means of feudal feofs: Godfrey of Bouillon, for example, was accompanied by a brother, Baldwin, Bohemond by a nephew, Tancred, who hoped to mend their fortunes overseas. To this galaxy of disappointed men we must add one great potentate, Raymond of Toulouse: we may note that even Raymond, who was endowed with immense territorial power in the south of France, attempted to carve himself out a principality in the East. It has been calculated that in all between four and five thousand knights went in one or other of the great armies. Many took their wives and families with them and clearly had no intention of coming home again. For every knight there were about five infantrymen.

With the details of the Crusade we cannot here concern ourselves. The 'Peoples' Crusade' of poor men, led by the preacher Peter the Hermit, was completely unexpected by the Emperor. Decimated on its journey through the Balkans, its members were finally massacred by the Turks at Civetot, between Nicomedia and Nicaea, in October 1096. The main armies converged on Constantinople in the early months of 1097, their way through imperial territories having been smoothed by the careful preparations of the emperor.[1] Alexius had, indeed, a difficult task. He wished to retain control over the crusaders and over any conquests they should make. As it was, the crusading leaders only swore loyalty to him with bad grace and in return for large bribes. The wealth of Constantinople itself led to marauding by undisciplined knights. The luxury and sophistication of the court baffled and frustrated the illiterate and scheming nobles from the West.

The Crusade itself illustrated the cupidity already shown by the barons and it also demonstrated the reality of their spiritual convictions. For the essential point is that, despite difficult siege operations for which they lacked materials, terrible hunger and thirst which led to many desertions, and the onset of diseases produced by excessive heat and unfamiliar food, the armies finally reached, captured, and sacked Jerusalem in July 1099. On the way there Bohemond had made himself prince of Antioch, Baldwin had

[1] The recruiting stage in Europe was accompanied by widespread persecution of the Jews, especially in the Rhineland, for it was believed that the Jews in Jerusalem had helped to betray the city to the Turks.

carved himself out a principality at Edessa, and many a smaller man had feathered his nest both from captured Turkish booty and the feofs and lordships bestowed by the successful magnates. Jerusalem itself was made into a kingdom to which Godfrey of Bouillon was elected; on his death shortly afterwards he was followed as king by Baldwin. The fourth and final territory to be acquired was Tripoli, captured in 1109, and given as a county to Bertrand, son of Raymond of Toulouse. In all the Latin principalities feudal relationships were at once established. The merchants of Genoa, Venice, and Pisa hastened to supply the new masters of the Syrian coast. A vast area had been conquered and even wider fields of expansion seemed to offer themselves, east to Damascus, south to Alexandria, Cairo, and the fabulous wealth of the Nile valley.

The conquests were, however, superficial: internal conflict among the Turks had alone permitted the crusaders to advance, and the moment the opposition was united the Syrian principalities were doomed. The eastern emperors were jealous and suspicious. The Christian principalities were themselves often at loggerheads with each other. The traders in the coastal cities were not anxious for an aggressive policy such as was advocated by the two great military monastic Orders, the Knights of the Temple and of the Hospital,[1] which were soon richly endowed in Europe and in the Near East to prosecute the Holy War. Edessa fell in 1144, and the great leader Saladin recaptured Jerusalem and nearly all

---

[1] Or Knights of St. John. Though assimilated to monks, members of the military Orders were technically laymen.

the Holy Land in 1187. The Second and Third Crusades (1147-9, 1191-2) failed miserably to recover lost land. Led by kings who quarrelled, dominated by the Italian shipping interests responsible for conveying many of the armies to their destination, these later crusades only achieved the recapture of Acre (which did not fall again until 1291) and the occupation of the Byzantine island of Cyprus which henceforth became the headquarters of the 'kingdom of Jerusalem'. In 1204 the Fourth Crusade frankly abandoned the earlier programme. Largely under Venetian inspiration, the Crusaders attacked and captured Constantinople itself, which then had a Latin emperor until 1261. Rapacity and devotion had mingled in the First Crusade. By 1204 the very word crusade had lost its meaning.

We have followed briefly the external expansion of western chivalry in Spain, southern Italy, and the Near East. The northern and north-eastern expansion was undertaken more exclusively by Germans. It was both less dramatic and, in the long run, more permanent than the Syrian conquests. No ocean or mountain range obstructed German expansion and, from Charlemagne onwards, there was a steady push to the east and north. The effective limits of Germany in the time of Charlemagne were the River Elbe in the north and the upper waters of the River Danube in the east. Otto I's defeat of the Magyars in 955 was the signal for a further advance: the march of Austria was created, the kingdom of Bohemia (Slav by language) became tributary to the German king; and the lands between Saxony and the Oder were incorporated in the marcher defence system. This advance was not made without difficulty; under Otto II, for instance, the Slavs between Elbe and Oder successfully threw off imperial control. But by Henry III's reign (d. 1056) the young kingdoms of Poland and Hungary for a time recognized German suzerainty and in the reign of Frederick I Barbarossa (d. 1190) very rapid progress was made, particularly under the leadership of Henry the Lion, duke of Saxony and Bavaria, and Albert the Bear. Holstein and Mecklenberg were gradually Germanized and so was extensive territory beyond the Oder.

As the Crusade in the Near East lost its attraction, so the battle against the pagans in the Baltic area increased in vehemence. The Teutonic Order of knights, established, like the Orders of Templars and Hospitallers, for service against the Turks, transferred its attentions to the Prussians in the early thirteenth century, joining with another German order, the Knights of the Sword, in 1237. The primitive peoples of the coastland from Prussia to the Gulf of Finland were gradually reduced to dependence, and the conquered areas were ruled autocratically by the knights, whose forbidding monastic castles surveyed a subjugated land. Soon only the heathen Lithuanians separated the Christian Poles and the territories of the Teutonic Order from the barbarous but Orthodox Christian Russians still farther to the east. The knights, ruled by an elected grand master responsible in theory to emperor and pope, were in fact independent and, though dedicated to the spreading of Christianity, did not hesitate occasionally to expand at the expense of Christian Poland.

By itself the *furor Teutonicus*, which sowed poisonous seeds of hatred to grow in later ages, might have been superficial enough. But in the wake of the knights, who were mainly drawn from the petty nobility of south Germany, came peasants, artisans, and traders from the north, while great bishoprics were established in dependence on the Order. This more peaceful penetration of Germans of both high and low degree also occurred in Poland, Bohemia, and Hungary, laying permanent foundations for German expansion eastwards.

The protracted campaigns on the borders of Christendom which have been touched on in the previous pages were of great significance for the future development of European society, and in no way more than by drawing off in successive generations so many turbulent younger sons who might otherwise have made trouble at home. The preoccupation of the more restless knights in distant campaigns did much to produce a more coherent sense of Christendom, of the fundamental similarities existing between French, English, Spaniards, and Germans, as against Wends, Balts, Turks, and Greeks. And it also aided the kings of Europe to make good their control over their subjects.

We have already considered the survival of monarchy during the Dark Ages and seen how kings depended on sanctified heredity and superior position in the feudal hierarchy. We must now consider the positive activity of kings, which was, even at this time, gradually giving them a point of view and a policy different to those of other great magnates. In these developments France is, so to speak, a test case for there feudal society had taken deeper root than elsewhere. The Norman kings of Sicily and England exhibited remarkable constitutional advance as a result of their position as the inheritors of conquered lands; the kings of Germany had, as we have seen, a tradition of public law on which they could draw. But in France we see the emergence of monarchy under less favourable circumstances.

The Capetians certainly possessed initial advantages in the disposition of their personal lands. Controlling Paris and Orleans, and holding the lordship over some great monasteries like Saint-Denis, they had a basis of territorial power which made them equal to all but the greatest of the dukes and counts who were nominally their vassals. At first, however, the dynasty 'vegetated', as has been well said. Save for ensuring the descent of the Crown and maintaining as far as possible control over churches and monasteries, Robert (d. 1031) and Henry I (d. 1060) took no aggressive steps to reinforce their authority, and were much less active than, for example, the contemporary rulers of Anjou (above, p. 115). The court was peripatetic, circulating from manor to manor. The royal entourage fluctuated in composition, but the clerks, barons, and bishops who accompanied the king, like those who attended full meetings of his vassals when he called them for advice as a feudal lord, could seldom interfere with the virtually independent dukes of Aquitaine and Normandy, counts of Barcelona, Toulouse, Gascony, Blois, Chartres, Anjou, and Flanders.

From the end of the eleventh century a more assertive attitude begins to be noticeable. French kings from Philip I (d. 1108) onwards were, in short, anxious to rule their vassals. From 1066 the duke of Normandy was king of England; a policy of weakening his hold on the great French feof was essential to the survival of the French monarchy, and the Crown found willing helpers in the neighbouring counts of Flanders and Anjou. A fresh intransigeance also marked the attitude of the Crown to the smaller vassals on the royal domain. After 1154 feudal dynasticism produced an even greater threat. Henry II of England disposed of French feofs greater in extent than those remaining under Capetian control: the Angevin 'Empire' included Normandy, Brittany, Anjou, Poitou, Aquitaine; it ran unbroken from the Channel in the north to the Pyrenees in the south, and in the centre stretched from the Atlantic almost to the Rhône. The danger that these possessions might lead to the English king swallowing France was real enough. Henry II and his nobles were French speaking; no 'national sentiment' existed to separate the English and the French; the issues were essentially dynastic, legal, and political. This second challenge was faced by the French kings of the twelfth century with even greater ingenuity and resource. In the course of the twelfth century France acquired rudimentary institutions which, though feudal in origin, were developed to distinctly non-feudal ends.

Even in the first period of royal development, in the reign of Louis VI (the 'Fat', d. 1137) there was a noticeable increase in the regularity with which the king's business was in the hands of relatively obscure clerks in his household. These men had no distracting loyalties and saw a strong Crown as the only way of securing that peace which, as Churchmen, they considered the supreme earthly good. The most remarkable of them, Suger, was the son of a serf who rose in 1122 to be abbot of Saint-Denis (d. 1151). He was Louis VI's right-hand man and occasionally put into words a novel view of the royal function: thus he can write of the king giving justice 'like an emperor' (*imperialiter*), he can equate the 'kingdom' with a more absolute idea of government (*regnum* and *respublica*). It was, however, under Philip II (*d.* 1223) and Louis IX (*d.* 1270), in the second period of development, that the concrete attributes of the crown began to match these aspirations.

The first step naturally came in the local government of the royal domain. Here, from about 1190, the provosts of the king, who had held their offices mainly as hereditary feofs, began to come under the control of 'bailifs' (*baillis*), officers of the Crown who had a supervisory charge over the royal *prévôts*, and who, under Louis IX, were themselves subjected to local inquests as a step to prevent them from becoming petty tyrants. The domain, thus more efficiently controlled, was made to yield a higher income. This, the 'ordinary' revenue of the Crown, consisted of a multitude of small rents from royal manors, forest rights and so forth, and it more than doubled during the reigns of Philip II, his son and his grandson. There was also a vast increase in profits from justice, from tolls, from licences to Jews and 'Lombards' (below, p. 160), and from periodic persecution of these 'usurers'. The Church yielded a regular income of gifts and of feudal income during the vacancies of abbeys and bishoprics. Above all, the Crusade became a royal responsibility and from the end of the twelfth century the principle was firmly established (though not without much grumbling) that the clergy and magnates not taking part in crusading activity should pay for those who were; and that the Crown should collect such funds. The use as a treasury of the Temple at Paris, headquarters in France of the Knights Templar, reveals this process at work. It was equally revealed by the wholesome growth of a mercenary army. Cash payment was essential in the thirteenth century for the creation of an army: 'When they hear that the king is paying well and largely, the knights will come from all parts', Joinville told Louis IX, and since cash could thus provide the elements of power, it is hardly surprising that Louis IX took pains to secure a stable coinage. which should prevail over the lesser currencies of his vassals.

Finally, the *curia regis*, the king's court, maintained its ability to deal with the ramifications of a more active royal administration. It was still augmented regularly into a great council, when the tenants-in-chief came to give their feudal overlord advice or counsel. But it also existed in the form of a narrower body, the *conseil secret* or *étroit*, the 'privy council' of expert members of the royal household, whose familiarity with day-to-day business ensured continuity and consistency of government. On the judicial side the *curia regis* was also developing into permanent form, in the shape of what was soon to be called the 'Parlement of Paris'; though the king still retained and exercised the right to summary jurisdiction, a body of professional lawyers existed in the 'Palais' to which the Crown habitually referred disputes, and to which the vaguely defined 'Peers of France' were attached as an indication that the older jurisprudence of feudalism, with its rule that a lord should be judged by his equals or peers, was not forgotten in this distinctly non-feudal development.

These changes did not take place without encountering resistance. Counts of Flanders, of Alsace, of Blois, and of Toulouse could and did turn their backs on the Crown and make compromising alliances with the king of England or the emperor of Germany. Even the prelates, most loyal supporters of Capetian aggrandizement, could be unco-operative, as when they compelled Philip II in 1189 to refer to crusading taxation (the 'Saladin Tithe') as 'outrageous' and 'not to be repeated'; or when they combined in an attempt to cow Louis IX. But there was an immense fund of goodwill on which the Crown could draw. The poor and the peasantry were foremost among those who stood to gain from an increase in royal power. The inhabitants of the rising towns (below, p. 147) were natural allies of the king. Even the lesser nobles often resented the brigandage of members of their own class. There must have been many smaller barons who echoed the sentiments of Hugh of Clermont, attacked by an ungrateful son-in-law in 1102: 'I would much rather, my dear lord', he said to Louis VI, 'that you should possess all my lands, since I hold them from you, than that my degenerate son-in-law (*gener degener*) should have them.' The squabbles on the domain naturally tended to the Crown's advantage; under Louis IX the reputation of royal justice was so high that litigants brought their cases from far afield, weakening in this way the powers of local magnates.

The chief efforts of the French monarchy were, of course, directed towards the struggle with England. Neither Philip II nor Louis IX were conscious of having any monarchical or 'anti-feudal' programme. Their innovations as described above were solely designed for *ad hoc* problems and were not part of a system. As it was, the victorious campaigns of Philip II against England, which were to earn him the title Augustus, were aided by a most effective use of all the old devices of feudal dynasticism—marriage alliances, encouragement of vassals disgruntled by Henry II's vigorous government, above all by the skilful use of Henry's disloyal sons. Even in this field success was due as much to good luck as to careful planning: it was Richard I of England's absence on Crusade and John's controversy with the papacy which enabled final victory to be won. The battle of Bouvines (1214) saw the end of the Angevin 'Empire'. By the Treaty of Paris (1259), negotiated between Louis IX and Henry III, the English kings henceforth held only the small duchy of Guyenne. For over a century the English magnates, who demonstrated in the Great Charter of 1215 their desire for a brake on royal power, were reluctant to embark on continental expeditions. Equally unpremeditated was the penetration of Capetian power into Provence, in the wake of the Albigensian 'crusaders' (above, p. 111). Nor was the French Crown original in its disposal of the great feofs it had recovered. Some were retained in the direct control of the king, but others were given as great appanages (literally = 'provisions') to members of the royal family—a policy which in the event was to prove immensely rewarding (below, p. 196), but which might have dismembered the country if it had not been accompanied by a growth of royal power.

Nothing could be more significant of Capetian *naïveté* at this stage than the willingness of kings to take the Cross. That Louis VII (*d*. 1180) did so in the Second Crusade (1147-9) is perhaps of small significance, for his activities in France were on a reduced scale. But Philip II Augustus also campaigned in the East (1190-1), though he shrewdly returned to take advantage of the absence of Richard I. The greatest crusader of all was Louis IX, whose resolute defence of Christendom and devout if frigid life led promptly to his canonization. St. Louis was in the East from 1248 to 1254. Such a lengthy absence would have been inconceivable if the king had been consciously engaged at home on a policy of strong government. It must also remind us that feudal relations could be stabilizing forces in society. St. Louis's absence was marked by no major troubles at home, where his mother acted as regent. In this connexion we must also recall that the kings of England never formally renounced their position as vassals of the Capetians for their French feofs, vast though these sometimes were. Both Crown and barons in France in the thirteenth century were content with the place of the monarchy in the feudal order, because neither was aware that it had changed.

The other kingdoms of western Europe had developed in somewhat different ways. England since 1066 had also demonstrated how feudalism could be employed to strengthen the hands of kings: it has indeed been argued that the Capetians we have been discussing deliberately aped the tricks of Normans and Plantagenets. England was conquered and planted with French barons, who naturally inclined to exalt the monarchy which alone guaranteed their territorial status, while the Crown was equally inclined to a judicious reliance on the counsel of the great magnates. As a result the magnates regularly attended the great council, thus paving the way for its extension into parliament. In the Spanish kingdoms, where reconquest was a permanent political aim, feudalism also, as in England, led to lively and original central institutions (below, p. 184), though civil war in and between the small kingdoms of the peninsula retarded the growth of royal power.

In the greatest of all western kingdoms, however, the relationship of vassal to lord did not reinforce the Crown. The power and prestige of German kings in the tenth and eleventh centuries have already occupied our attention and we have seen how the emperors disputed with contempory popes for control over the Church. The victory in that struggle had gone to the popes; though for long the emperors made full use of their practical power to dominate bishops and abbots and of their legal power (above, p. 99) to interfere in disputed elections. Indeed the mere need to compromise with the reforming papacy, which embarrassed the rulers of every country in the West, can hardly be advanced as the sole explanation of the gradual decline in German monarchy during the twelfth and thirteenth centuries. There were other underlying processes which must be briefly examined.

The emperor claimed authority at first not as a feudal lord but as the supreme ruler in Germany. But the public rights which he claimed were shared by the greater dukes and counts, whose hereditary right to such powers the emperors had to concede, compensating for an absence of feudal control over the laity by an endowment of the Church with military feofs which, as we have seen, was on a massive scale. The dukes and other great magnates associated their legal position with their dynastic territories, and tried to use what had been a military charge over the free men in the area into a territorial domination of all the inhabitants. Tenth- and eleventh-century emperors were able to prevent this programme from being fully accomplished, but they were powerless to prevent the close association of legal power and land at the level of the smaller baronage. Scattered widely over Germany, but most numerous in the centre and south, in Franconia, Swabia, and Bavaria, were scores of small dynasties straining every effort to turn their allodial lands (above, p. 52) into a secure domain protected by a castle (*Burgbezirk*, castellany) and augmented by the lands which were being constantly reclaimed from the forest (above, p. 119) royal rights over which could not be maintained by the distracted kings of the Investiture period. These factors—allodial land, internal colonization, and the fundamental assumption that possession of non-feudal estates conferred rights of government—were responsible for the development in Germany of a mass of powerful lords who were beyond the machinery of feudal control.

It was precisely to a more rigorously feudal type of control that the Hohenstauffen emperors turned as a substitute for the combination of public law plus mastery of the Church which had served their Saxon and Salian predecessors and which had been weakened by the struggle with the popes. The decision to use feudalism was, in a sense, forced upon the Hohenstauffen. The long conflict with Rome had encouraged every particularist element in Germany. The great magnates seized all opportunities of dominating lesser neighbours and insisting on feudal commendation and vassalage. The bishops acquired a new political independence equally expressed in feudal forms. The *ministeriales* secured the status of nobility and their feofs became hereditary. The main symbol of the changed position of the crown was the violent alteration in the dynasty procured more than once by papal intervention and the ambition of the German magnates, lay and clerical: the elections of 1077 (Rudolf of Swabia), 1125 (Lothar of Saxony,) 1138 (Conrad of Swabia) 'flouted legitimism' and in any case provoked civil war, which intensified a chaos in which lords could cement the practical power of castles and lands.

Under Frederick I (Barbarossa, d. 1190) the government of Germany was put on a new footing by accepting these developments. In his long reign Frederick aimed at the Capetian policies of using feudal relations to maintain control over the great magnates and of extending and exploiting the royal domain. As far as the first aspect of his government is concerned it may be seen in the privileges accorded to the dukes (like that of 1156, relieving the duke of Austria of all but nominal feudal services to the emperor). Such acts made the dukes for the first time genuine masters of all the subjects in their duchies, for which they were now in theory responsible, as tenants-in-chief, to the Crown. The second aspect may be illustrated by the retention of Swabia under direct control of royal officials when it escheated to the crown in 1168, and the establishment of royal control at Goslar in Saxony, an important administrative centre which was also rich in silver mines. The *regnum Italicum* seems to have fitted into this dynastic pattern, save that feudal controls were necessarily abandoned there and Frederick aimed to control Lombardy directly, like his domain lands in Germany. This he failed to do, despite a series of expensive campaigns in Italy (1158–62, 1166–7, 1174–7), and he had to be content with an Italian domain concentrated in the much less wealthy Tuscany, ruled by imperial lieutenants and supported by a marriage alliance with the Normans in Sicily: his son Henry married the Norman heiress Constance in 1186.

Yet in all respects the programme of Frederick I miscarried. His Italian policy not only flouted the ambitions of the towns of Lombardy, where he was defeated in battle by the townsmen at Legnano in 1176, but terrified the papacy with its threat of encirclement—a threat which became a reality when his successors Henry VI (*d.* 1197) and Frederick II (*d.* 1250) made it clear that they intended to be Sicilian kings and rule northern Italy from a secure base in the south. The popes of the late twelfth and early thirteenth centuries exerted themselves to provoke German opposition to their oppressive Hohenstauffen neighbours; Innocent III found the kings of France and England equally anxious to seek allies in Germany at the expense of the emperor. As a result, there were electoral disputes soon after Barbarossa died and these lasted intermittently even after Frederick II's accession in 1212.

Equally unsuccessful was the feudal policy within Germany. On the one hand it was powerless against the allodial tradition. When Henry the Lion, duke of Saxony and Bavaria, stubbornly resisted the emperor's attempts to reduce his power in the north,

Frederick I could defeat him and deprive him of his two great duchies, but he could not strip him of his allodial lands; as master of Brunswick and Lüneburg, Henry was still a magnate capable of hurting the emperor. On the other hand, the rights which the emperor gave the greater magnates redounded to their power and prestige rather than his the moment he failed to impress them with his superiority. Italy made him vulnerable to their pressure and later emperors were compelled to make concessions, like the 'Statute in favour of the Princes' of 1232 which went far to turn *de facto* into *de jure* independence. As early as 1199 at Speyer the magnates announced the ominous principle that the prince elected by the other princes was automatically emperor, a doctrine finally settled in 1338 and 1356 (below, p. 198).

From the death of Frederick II there was no emperor worth the name in Germany for a quarter of a century. When the title was resumed, the office had lost everything but the memory of its early splendour. Thus the twelfth and thirteenth centuries in Germany produced developments which were to make the German monarchy negligible as a political force for the next half millennium. The Germany of the princes (*principes imperii*, *Reichsfürsten*) had arrived. It is hardly to be wondered at that during this period of decline a natural euphemism added the adjective 'holy' to the Roman Empire in the West. The 'Holy Roman Empire' was to last until 1806; genuine kingship in Germany was already a memory by 1250.

We must close by again stressing that German kings, like French kings (above, p. 139), were hardly conscious of the 'programmes' which historians necessarily read into their actions. Frederick I acted from day to day in the best interests of his dynasty; 'feudalism' was a word as yet uninvented. Just as St. Louis's crusade is a sufficient commentary on the artlessness of his aggrandizement, so is Frederick I's. Taking the Cross in 1188, Frederick finally set out from Ratisbon at Easter 1189, and he was drowned in Cilicia in June 1190. To us this seems an astonishing withdrawal from responsibilities; to contemporaries it set the seal on Frederick's grandeur. Boisterous, learned, a doughty champion of royal rights in Germany and Italy, his crusading death was a crowning glory.

The times were passing when kings could take their duties so lightly. When St. Louis set out for Tunis in 1270 on his last ill-fated expedition he failed to convince Joinville, the seneschal of Champagne who had chronicled the earlier campaigns of his master, of the wisdom of another crusade. 'I held', wrote Joinville, 'that all men who advised the king to go on this expedition committed mortal sin; for at the point at which France then was, all the kingdom was at good peace with itself and its neighbours, while ever since he departed, the state of the kingdom has done nothing but go from bad to worse.' Joinville himself, a layman writing a vernacular language, was one sign that a new society was in process of creation. To this new society we must now turn.

Part III From Christendom to Europe

CHAPTER VI

THE TOWNS

Development of commerce; political and social development of the towns town politics in Italy; Hanseatic League; Swiss Confederation; general social consequences of commerce.

BY the ninth century the old Roman towns, most numerous in the provinces bordering the Mediterranean, had sadly declined from their earlier importance, while in northern Europe town life, even of the relatively superficial Roman type, had never developed. The Roman towns had been primarily administrative centres: commerce and trade in Roman times were limited, as we have seen. Power in the later Empire lay with the potentates scattered in rural areas, who merged naturally into the feudal order of the following age. During the centuries after 800 that comparative security and stability which had led to a marked growth of population also permitted the development of trade on a gradually increasing scale. Trade brought fresh life to the moribund civic communities of the South, and in the North it created towns where none had existed before. With some consequences of this we have already had to concern ourselves: the change from services to rent on the manor is one of the most significant results of the process. By the thirteenth century the development of towns had reached a point where the whole temper of western European society had been radically affected.

The contrast between the money economy of Europe in and after the thirteenth century and the 'natural' economy of the previous epoch was greatly exaggerated by historians and economists a hundred years ago. We now realize that money and money values were never abandoned even during the darkest parts of the Dark Ages. A later generation, while admitting the survival of cash as a medium of exchange, overstressed the interruption of trade occasioned by the later invasions of Moslems and Norsemen. This view, associated with the great Belgian historian Pirenne, was in turn criticized, and evidence has accumulated that the merchant was active, even in northern Europe, during the least propitious times between 800 and 1000, that the Mediterranean, although it became 'a Moslem lake', continued to bear Christian ships. Yet, when all allowances have been made, the ninth, tenth, and eleventh centuries form a period when commerce was at a singularly low ebb: the dominant position of the landed magnate is proof, if proof were needed, that there was then no rival to land as a source of wealth and power.

The first change in this situation came in the South. The maritime cities of Italy continued to trade with Byzantium, which, as already noted (above, p. 124), was an important terminus of the Asiatic trade routes. From Naples, Amalfi, and Bari in the south of the Italian peninsula, and from Venice at the head of the Adriatic, ships sailed along the

THE TOWNS 149

shores of Greece to reach the Sea of Marmora. The Norman conquest of Naples and Sicily left Venice as the most important of these ports and soon Venetian merchants were trading not only with Constantinople where by 1082 they were exempt from imperial taxation, but with the Moslems in North Africa and Syria. This commercial activity turned Venice into a wealthy and powerful city. Situated on lagoons, she was easily defended against attack from the mainland where at first she possessed only a narrow strip of territory. The example of Venice was not lost on the smaller ports of the western coast of Italy, and by the eleventh century the shipping of Pisa and Genoa began to take an ever larger part in Mediterranean trade. When the First Crusade captured a large part of the Syrian coast the future of Christian trade was assured. One of Bohemond's first acts after he acquired Antioch was to give a monopoly there to the merchants of Genoa. Marseilles and Barcelona were soon sharing in this commerce with the Latin Orient and the mounting control over the Crusades exercised by shipping interests tells its own story, culminating in the Fourth Crusade and the Latin Empire at Constantinople (above, p. 131). The flow of trade percolated beyond the ports: Venetian prosperity spread through the valley of the Po and over the Alpine passes; Pisa fructified Florence and Lucca and other Tuscan towns; while from Genoa and Marseilles the new activity of money and merchants spread through Provence and up the valley of the Rhône.

Northern trade also owed much to contact with Constantinople. The Norse adventurers who passed down the Dnieper (above, p. 35), acted as a channel of trade between the Baltic and the Black Sea,[1] and 'great hoards of Islamic and Greek coins' have been found on the island of Gothland, evidently 'the great entrepôt of this traffic and its point of contact with northern Europe'. The shores of the North Sea were exploited as assiduously and, in the wake of Norse invasion and settlement, trading-posts were established at many points on the west coast of Germany, as well as in England, Scotland, and Ireland. Here again the impulse of trade soon made itself felt in adjacent areas. By the end of the eleventh century flourishing communities of traders are found in the river valleys of western Germany and France. Hamburg on the Elbe, Cologne and Mainz on the Rhine, Rouen and Paris on the Seine are only the most important of many such centres, while the smaller rivers of the Low Countries, the Scheldt and the Meuse, permitted the development of trading stations at Cambrai and Ghent, at Liége, Dinant, and Verdun, while Bruges, then connected directly with the sea, acquired growing importance, as did the port of London.

The commodities involved in this increasing commerce varied according to their origin. The trade of the eastern Mediterranean consisted at first of exports of slaves (see above, p. 59 n.), iron and timber, in return for which the Italian merchants brought home silk, spices and drugs, precious metals and finely wrought articles of decoration and adornment. The northern trade dealt in furs, honey, fish. Moreover commodities produced within western Europe itself were already the object of distant exchange.

[1] The Volga route to Astrakhan and the Caspian was also followed.

Wine from the favoured valleys of Guyenne, Burgundy, and the Rhineland early circulated far afield, and the fustians of Lombardy bore witness to a specialized cloth production which was even more signally developed in the woollen manufacture of Flanders and Florence.

Once imported or produced, the articles of commerce laboriously journeyed with their dealers towards the markets where they were exchanged and sold. The routes they followed were overland and, midway between the two great inland seas, merchants congregated at the fairs of Champagne to display their wares. A succession of famous markets at Lagny-sur-Marne, Bar, Provins, and Troyes gave traders the chance to meet one another for most of the year. Subsidiary fairs were held in many more distant places and in general the small intrinsic importance of many of the fair-towns is a useful reminder that they did not represent a local market: they were occasions when merchants dealt with merchants, under the protection of the local lord who gained financially from the concourse of visiting traders.

The goods thus brought from one end of Europe to the other were finally sold to those who could afford them. In southern Europe many nobles lived in the old cities and this was an added reason for the rapidity with which commerce revitalized the towns of the Mediterranean area. In the North the merchant made his way to the largest groups of consumers he could find—the small 'cities' where bishops had their sees and where a numerous retinue of priests and servants resided; the monasteries, where the monks were not averse to refining their way of life; the great castles of the magnates and their families and retainers. The towns of the South and the strong places of the North thus attracted the merchant and his stock-in-trade.

More important than that, in such places he began to make a permanent settlement. In the old towns he acquired land and built himself a house which was at once his home, his office, and his warehouse. Soon the Roman foundations—shrunk sometimes so small that all the inhabitants huddled, as at Nîmes, within the walls of the amphitheatre—began to swell again not merely to cover the original Roman area but to sprawl beyond it. In the North new towns appeared where none had yet been seen. A few plots of land inside the *enceinte* of the cathedral, inside the abbey wall, or the outer defences of the castle or *burg* did not suffice for long to contain the merchants, their families and hangers-on. Soon the cluster of roofs was more numerous outside than inside the original establishment. Once started, if conditions were favourable, the agglomeration grew like a snowball. The inn-keepers, porters, servants multiplied and soon the butchers, bakers, and candlestick-makers, the smiths, carpenters, and masons added their services and created new consumer demands. Before long the town was given a wall for defence, became itself a *burg* or fortified place, and its inhabitants were described as *burgenses*, the dwellers in the *burg*, the bourgeoisie.

The birth of the bourgeoisie was painful everywhere, even in the towns of southern France and of Italy, but nowhere was it more painful than in the northern homeland of feudalism. An instinctive distrust sprang up between the possessors of landed

THE TOWNS 153

wealth on the one hand and on the other the new class of traders and the bourgeois groups which the traders had so largely created. That the rich magnate was increasingly dependent on the merchant for his wine and his sword, as well as for his pepper and the silks and jewels of his womenfolk, did not lessen the tension. Nor did the encroachment made by the town on his lands, which deprived him of the old income and services of the manor, do more than alleviate his financial embarrassment for a short time, for he found that the *burgenses* were prepared to buy privileges from him once and once only and violently resisted his attempts to mulct them at will. There was an added irritation in the happy relationship into which the lord's feudal superior was prepared to enter with the town and fear of the danger that the town and the Crown between them might squeeze lesser lords out of the picture. Nor was the lord's dislike of burgesses entirely due to the threat they represented to his power and prestige. The official teaching of the Church viewed the merchant's activities with contemptuous distaste, as we shall see (below, p. 219). The clergy constantly hissed their terrified disapproval: 'a bloated swelling of the people, a terror of the kingdom, a wet blanket on the church', wrote an English monk in the twelfth century. His continental contemporaries shared these sentiments, which made the merchant and the citizen uncomfortable and fortified the active hostility of lords of land.

The wall with which the new *burg* was surrounded had to be paid for, it had to be maintained and it had to be manned. This involved an organization, however rudimentary. The principal burgesses in assembly jointly undertook these charges together with a further programme—the emancipation of all inhabitants of the town from the control of the lord, the responsibility of the town as a whole for the taxes and dues laid on its members, the administration of law within the walls by magistrates chosen by the burgesses and not the bailiff or steward appointed by the lord. To these ends the burgesses bound themselves by oath, thus establishing what contemporaries called a commune and (in a fine phrase) 'substituting an oath of loyalty between equals for the feudal oath of obedience to a superior'. Little by little the audacious plan was realized. Lords, or their superiors, granted charters when faced with private difficulties or public danger. Many northern towns were given charters of privilege by 1100, and a century later the 'enfranchised burgh' was as common as formerly it had been rare. The towns, fortified, administering their own law, were self-conscious islands of 'liberties', that is, of specific exemptions from the normal operation of manor and feof. No more momentous event has occurred in European history than this. For the 'liberty' of the town gradually became a status applicable to all its inhabitants. The urban groups established that to dwell in a town for a year and a day conferred 'freedom' on any man, even a serf.

The change was accomplished more readily on lands held by the laity, most readily of all on the domain of kings, who were always readier to sell immunities and who shared the bourgeois aims of peace and safe communications. Thus on the Capetian lands many communes were established and in England the monarchs were also willing to encourage civic growth. But in Church centres the clergy proved more doughty opponents and there the burgesses had more often to fight harder. In Italy, in the towns of Tuscany and Lombardy, the German emperors did their best to maintain the position of their nominated bishops, but to no avail. The civil power passed to the citizens, and after Frederick I's defeat at Legnano (above, p. 144) the Italian commune flourished almost unimpeded as far as external pressures were concerned. The external threat was not, however, the only danger encountered by the town. The thirteenth and fourteenth centuries witnessed civil strife in many urban communities except where (as in France and England) strong royal supervision intervened.

The first grant of privilege had been secured by the rich merchants acting in concert. A few families in each centre had thrived on the long-distance trade, acquired property in the town and monopolized its government (its 'lordship', *échevinage* in Flanders, *signoria* in Italy). These 'patricians', as they have been well named, were not anxious to share their powers with the steadily mounting numbers of citizens of more modest rank. These, the 'middle class' of the towns, were composed of the craftsmen who satisfied the needs of a local market, working for the most part with local materials. Organized in corporations (craft-guilds, Fr. *métiers*, Ital. *arti*) in order to protect the members by restricting entry and providing mutual support in sickness or trouble, and to protect the consumer by ensuring consistent standards and fair prices,[1] the masters in each craft

[1] The doctrine of the 'just price' seems to have first been mooted in episcopal cities. It was seldom more than an aspiration, though later sanctioned by public opinion.

were the heads of small economic units. The master's shop was usually in his house. There his apprentices worked for him and so did those apprentices who had qualified and who remained as day-labourers (journeymen), awaiting their chance of becoming masters. The master-butchers or master-joiners were thus small fry compared with the patricians, entrenched in town government, in 'grand commerce', and in the best property. But numerically they were important, and in their struggle with the patricians for a share in government they would sometimes enlist the support of higher authority—the chapter against the bishop, the prince against the local lord.

The success of the craft-guilds varied. In some places they won an outright victory—as at Liége, where all thirty-two guilds had equal representation on the city council by the middle of the fourteenth century; or at Cologne, where the guilds were finally victorious fifty years later. These, it will be noted, were both episcopal towns. Elsewhere in Germany the patricians were sometimes successful in holding their position: Nuremberg is an instance of this from south Germany and there are other similar towns in the north (cf. below, p. 168); or else patricians and guilds shared power, as they did by the beginning of the fifteenth century at Dortmund, Münster, and Osnabrück. In the wealthy weaving towns of Flanders similar compromises were effected by a system of 'members' which allocated representation on the council in a manner which reflected the economic and social importance of the various groups in the civic community. At Bruges by the mid-fourteenth century there were nine 'members': the patricians (the *poorterie*), the drapery crafts, butchers and fishmongers, metal-working crafts, leather-working crafts, cloth-making-up crafts, bakers, brokers, and finally one representing seventeen less-important guilds.

In the Italian towns civic politics had been bedevilled by 'Guelf' and 'Ghibelline' loyalties—a mere cloak by the fourteenth century for local family feuds[1]—and by the internal character of the struggle between the patricians (*grassi*) and petty nobility (*grandi*), for the latter lived inside the town rather than outside the walls, as in northern Europe. These troubles were to lead, as we shall shortly observe, to a relatively short period of genuine independence for many Italian communes, but in two great centres we can find developments parallel to those in Germany and Flanders. At Venice, for instance, the craft-guilds were of no importance at all and the patrician class, numerous and in general prepared to subordinate private gain to the prosperity of the Republic, dominated the city. These Venetian 'nobles' were a close hereditary corporation by the end of the thirteenth century. The doge (*dux*, duke) was elected for life by an elaborate process which prevented any one family from organizing a caucus to secure the office. But while the doge was surrounded with ever-growing pomp and circumstance real power was by 1335 in the hands of a council of ten (the *dieci*), elected annually by the 'nobility'. At

[1] These party-names go back to the period of active imperial intervention in Italy, especially during the mid-thirteenth century. Supporters of the emperor were Ghibellines (from a Hohenstauffen battle-cry), supporters of the pope were Guelfs (from the Welf opponents of the Hohenstauffen in Germany). There was at first a rough correspondence between the patrician merchants and the Guelfs, and between the nobility and the Ghibellines.

Florence the patricians and craft-guilds shared power, with the patricians predominating. There were twenty-one guilds in all, of which seven (the *arti maggiori*) represented big business—the import-export merchants, bankers, wool and silk merchants, lawyers, notaries, doctors of medicine and other respectable tradesmen, while the remaining fourteen guilds were those of the humdrum craftsmen. At Venice the constitution was designed to prevent any non-'noble' from acquiring public office. At Florence the machinery of government completely excluded the nobility: only a member of a guild could take part in the *signoria*, the supreme executive which was changed every two months, or in the various committees and advisory councils, which were elected for periods almost as short.[1]

In a few centres, where large-scale industry developed, a further stage took place: a proletariat challenged the guilds and the patricians. In certain Flemish towns (Bruges, Ypres, and Ghent), in Florence, and, to a lesser degree, in Cologne, the manufacture of cloth on a very big scale led to the existence of large numbers of poorly paid artisans—weavers, fullers, and dyers—engaged by small masters for short periods, at the mercy of any interruption of raw material supply (mainly English wool) or of the international market for the finished product.[2] Totally excluded from all government in the towns where they worked and to which they contributed much prosperity, it was natural that the workers (the 'blue nails' of Flanders, the *Ciompi* of Florence)

[1] It is impossible to indicate briefly the complexity of the Florentine constitution, which was frequently modified.
[2] Silk manufacture at Lucca, copper at Dinant, led to much the same situation.

should try to improve their social position. Strikes and lock-outs were common in these centres from the thirteenth century and in the fourteenth temporarily successful revolutions by the cloth-workers occurred in the Low Countries (1328, 1337, 1379) and in Florence (1378). Often the lesser guilds allied with the workers in these attempts to overthrow the richer citizens: but the violence of the workers always alienated all moderates and the impossibility of maintaining supplies of wool and selling the cloth without the help of the capitalist class always made the insurrections sterile and short-lived. In any case by the fifteenth century England had begun to manufacture woollen cloth instead of exporting the wool, and the importance of the continental woollen industry declined. This decline was intensified by the short-sighted and restrictive control of trade exercised by patricians or crafts or both. A policy of beggar-my-neighbour was as far as the city councils could go and it proved crippling to the prosperity of many towns.

By the fourteenth century, when these upheavals occurred, the merchant dealing with the 'international' market was very different from his twelfth-century predecessor. The latter had travelled to his customers and the great fairs, using the overland routes described (above, p. 150). Now the bigger traders were sedentary, they formed trading companies with permanent offices and depots in the principal cities of the West, and increasingly they used the sea. In these developments the Italians set the pace. By 1300 representatives of Italian merchant companies, based largely on family associations at home, were found everywhere north of the Alps—lending money at heavy rates of interest to princes (and recouping themselves by collecting the princes' revenues), transmitting cash and credit by bills of exchange from London to Avignon or Rome, from Hamburg to Barcelona, making their profits by engaging in the purchase and sale of commodities as well as in loans and exchange of currency. In certain important centres 'exchangers' operated and their facilities for handling currency soon developed in such a way that they were used by citizens and local magnates for settling accounts by means of ledger transactions; in Bruges all persons of substance had the equivalent of a bank account. At a lower level the pawn-shop business was developed as the bank of the poor, the 'Lombard Street' of many a western city commemorating this humble activity. The sea routes replaced the land routes not only because of political instability, but because the volume of trade increased. Genoese shipping was regularly making for Bruges by the end of the thirteenth century and Venetian galleys followed suit in the early fourteenth century.

In areas where strong monarchies were developing —England, France, Spain—the town and the Crown proved fruitful allies. The relative absence of strife between patricians and craft-guilds in these countries is no doubt mainly due to this. What was the fate of the towns in those parts of Christendom where the monarch was weak or entirely absent, Germany and Italy?

The Italian case calls for consideration first since urban development was more precocious there and because the Italian towns were less hampered by external pressures than those in the North. For the

THE TOWNS 161

greater part of the period between 1250 and 1450 there were no strong monarchs in Italy. We have seen that the Hohenstauffen attempt to found a powerful State in Italy was fruitless: Innocent III (*d.* 1216) and Innocent IV (*d.* 1254) were able to frustrate the policies of Frederick II (above, p. 144). Succeeding popes sought support far afield for their campaigns against Manfred, Frederick's illegitimate son, and finally found an able champion in Charles of Anjou (*d.* 1285). True, in some ways the cure was worse than the disease: Charles was an efficient and ambitious ruler; his aims embraced northern Italy as well as Sicily and Naples; and the establishment of his grandchildren in Hungary and the Adriatic area is evidence of his aggressive designs on eastern Europe. But Charles and his successors were embarrassed by a revolt in Sicily ('Sicilian Vespers', 1282) which placed the island more or less permanently under rulers of the Aragonese dynasty who, in the fifteenth century, extended their control to the mainland. In the centre of Italy lay the vast estates of the Church, running from Rome across to the Adriatic and extended northwards in 1279 by the acquisition of the Romagna. Here the successors of St. Peter had lands of great potential wealth. But their resources were more than absorbed by their struggle in the south. From 1305 to 1378, moreover, the popes were at Avignon (below, p. 177); thereafter to 1417 the papacy was weakened by the schism (below, p. 185). Hence no consistently effective rule was exercised over central Italy by the papacy for close on two centuries. Finally the rightful ruler of the *regnum Italicum*, the German emperor, was in no state to enforce his will in the north after the collapse of the Hohenstauffen. Fourteenth- and fifteenth-century emperors occasionally made the journey to Rome: Lewis IV, indeed, made a pitiful show of emulating a Henry III or a Barbarossa. But the connexion was now mainly formal and Frederick III (d. 1493) was the last emperor to be crowned in Rome.

Not merely had the Italian communes a free hand: the rivals for Italy as a whole, popes and emperors, Angevins and Aragonese, made bids for their support which at every point flattered civic self-esteem and extended civic privileges. Furthermore, the leagues of cities which had resisted Frederick I offered the framework of an organization which might have turned Italy from the Arno to the Alps into a federation of republican communes. Yet, with few exceptions, communal liberty was of short duration. Town after town during the half-century pivoting on 1300 succumbed to rule by a dynastic lord and saw its *signoria* in the hands of one man. The development may be illustrated from Milan, an illustrious but not untypical example.

At Milan in the thirteenth century the merchant classes (Guelf) united under the lead of the Della Torre family to resist the nobles (Ghibellines). The latter were led by Ottone Visconti, archbishop of Milan, who secured the expulsion of the Guelf leaders in 1278 and set about creating a permanent Ghibelline ascendancy based on a Visconti monopoly of power. As early as 1287 his great nephew Matteo was elected 'Captain of the People', and when Ottone died in 1295 Matteo succeeded as master of the city. The Della Torre managed to reassert themselves from 1302 to 1311, but in that year Matteo Visconti was again supreme, and he was made Imperial Vicar-General by the Emperor Henry VII. From that point Visconti power remained more or less undisturbed for nearly a century. Matteo (d. 1322) was followed by his two sons, Galeazzo (d. 1327) and Archbishop Giovanni (d. 1354), whence the succession fell to two nephews, Bernabò and Galeazzo II. The latter died in 1378 and his son Giangaleazzo, murdering Bernabò in 1385, turned *de facto* into *de jure* power when in 1395 he obtained from the emperor the title 'duke' at a cost of 100,000 florins.

The Della Scala at Verona, the Este at Ferrara, the Carrara at Padua, the Polenta at Ravenna have similar origins, though a less spectacular dominion; a score of other towns could produce parallel dynasties. Everywhere the pattern was much the same. A strong middle-class merchant group faced a strong petty nobility. One or other, or both (often in alliance with pope or emperor), in order to secure itself, committed leadership to an individual who was elected 'Captain of the People', 'Captain of the Merchants'—some existing office being used as a peg on which to hang autocracy and justify the proscription of opponents. Once the individual was invested with office a crisis enabled him first to magnify the authority of his magistracy, then to extend it in time, first for a period of years and afterwards indefinitely. A son or nephew meanwhile was 'elected' to office and inherited the control of the machinery of town government, staffed by junior members of the house and its clients. Thus the constitution remained, but was manipulated by a dynast who finally sought to legitimize his power by alliance with either of the two impecunious but universal monarchs, the pope or the emperor. Moreover the fighting was no longer carried out by citizen-soldiers, but by mercenary troops under *condottiere* captains (Lat. *conductor* = a contractor) who themselves entered the arena of territorial competition. It was, indeed, such a captain, Francesco Sforza, who in 1450 acquired the lordship of Milan.

The rise of lords in the greater communes entailed the subjugation by them of neighbouring cities. Here again Milan offers useful evidence. Even before the Visconti achieved power, Napoleone della Torre extended Milanese rule to Lodi, Novara, Como, Bergamo, and Brescia. These towns, and the large rural area or *contado* surrounding each, were permanently under Visconti rule, as were Cremona, Parma, Piacenza, Tortona, and Vercelli. Giovanni Visconti added for a time a band of territory from Nice to Genoa and Porto Venere, as well as broad lands round Asti and Alba. He and Giangaleazzo both dominated Bologna at different times, and Giangaleazzo's lordship extended to Pisa and its neighbourhood, to Siena, Verona, Vicenza, and Padua, besides extensive territories in the foot-hills of the Alps. In these cities the Visconti allowed local institutions to survive, maintaining their rule by partisans placed in key positions.

The empire of the Visconti engulfed more than a score of communes and absorbed lesser families of rulers in its stride. A succession of such ambitious houses rose and fell. Before the Visconti attained to the height of their power the Este of Ferrara and the Della Scala of Verona had acquired the rule of enormous areas of North Italy. After 1400 it was the turn of Florence and Venice to expand. In turning to this we shall see that the territorial expansion of the Este, Della Scala, and Visconti was due not simply to the swollen appetites of dynastic princes but was a process which was exemplified just as much by the two great republics.

In the course of the twelfth and thirteenth centuries Florentine territory was greatly extended. The original *contado* had a radius of about twenty miles. By 1400 this had been extended to about fifty, and Pistoia, Arezzo, and Volterra were among the chief places acquired; Lucca and Siena, earlier trade rivals, were now geographically as well as economically immobilized, though their total incorporation remained an aim of Florentine politics. Early in the fifteenth century Florence acquired Cortona, defeated (1406) her ancient rival Pisa, and secured Leghorn (Livorno) from Genoa. These advances were all made when Florence was in every sense a republic. Later additions, made when the Medici family was supreme in the city under Cosimo (d. 1464) and Lorenzo (d. 1492), conformed more nearly to dynastic expansion of the orthodox kind and were trifling by comparison. The truth was that the Italian city needed desperately to expand its *contado* so long as it was flourishing, in order to guarantee trade routes and provide food supplies for the citizens. The extended *contado*, vulnerable to the devastating attacks of *condottiere* armies, could only be protected by being buttressed by yet further territories.

Venice, where no dynastic family emerged, is an even better example. Originally basic necessities for the city were provided by narrow strips of mainland north and south of the lagoons. As the size of the city expanded, above all as powerful principalities developed on the mainland, it proved essential to take in the Trevigiano (Treviso and its neighbourhood) and a wide band of Istrian coastland south of Trieste. These spacious lands were in Venetian hands by the end of the fourteenth century. They proved untenable without further protection: Vicenza, Verona, and Padua, with all their surrounding areas, were absorbed, together with Friuli, in the first quarter of the fifteenth century; the next three decades saw Brescia and Bergamo added to the west. By the end of the century Venice had dominated all Italy north of the Po from Lake Como to the Isonzo, quite apart from her empire on the eastern shores of the Adriatic and in the Aegean. These strides were made hesitantly: conservatives at Venice deplored a policy which rooted Venice to terra firma and seemed to contradict or even to jeopardize the maritime sources of the city's prosperity. Yet each crisis made the process of aggrandizement more inevitable and demonstrated the weakness as well as the power of the Venetian State.

In these ways the Italian communes succumbed. By the end of the fifteenth century only Venice could truly be said to retain its original republican life, and even there a ruthless tyranny represented the dominance of the class of noble merchants. In Germany the evidence, though in some respects dissimilar, equally illustrates the growing power of princes.

As we have observed (above, p. 149) the Baltic and the Rhine were both trade routes of importance. Here towns of great wealth grew up and, particularly in the old Franconian and Swabian lands, many cities were privileged by the emperors and acquired complete independence as Imperial Free Cities (*Reichsfreistädte*). Such towns, when favoured by weak neighbours, could extend the area of their control more easily than those enfranchised by a lesser lord or a bishop. True, the princes forced Frederick II to renounce a traditional royal alliance with the towns which might have reinforced the monarchy, and city leagues proved short-lived and incapable of developing into permanent federations. Nevertheless many Free Cities survived both the coalitions of princes and the bands of predatory knights who were being hemmed in by both towns and princes: in 1521 no fewer than eighty-three were summoned to send representatives to the Reichstag (below, p. 198) of that year. Yet the cities which thus lingered on (and some retained a separate constitutional status until our own day) did so without much influence on general political development in Europe, while the territorial prince of the fifteenth century, from Flanders to Brandenburg, ruthlessly reduced the independence of the towns on his own domains, often intervening to his own advantage in the struggles between patricians and craft-guilds (*Zünftekämpfe*). Berlin itself, destined to become one day the capital of Germany, lost its independence in 1442 to a Hohenzollern margrave who answered only too willingly a call from the commons for help against the aldermen.

On the northern and southern edges of Germany there grew up, however, two associations which, perhaps because they were not town leagues of an orthodox kind, proved long-lived. The Hanseatic League and the Swiss Confederation, both of which emerge during the thirteenth century, exhibited a vigour and adaptability foreign to other town alliances in Germany. The Hanse remained influential until the sixteenth century and the Swiss Confederation was to develop into a permanent Republic.

The principal towns of northern Germany, Lübeck, and Hamburg, and Wisby on the island of Gothland, were ruled in the early thirteenth century by patrician families (*Geschlechter*) whose wealth derived from extensive trade in the Baltic and with Norway, Flanders, and England (above, p. 150). The first form which the Hanse (= company or fellowship) took was an association between these patrician trading families. By the mid-fourteenth century the association was between towns rather than families, although this is a somewhat unreal distinction if one remembers that the patrician families in most cases ruled the towns and that one of the subsidiary functions of the Hanse was to stamp out any popular constitutional change in a member-town. By the mid-fourteenth century the Hanse had added many other towns to the original nucleus round Lübeck, and in various ways and at various times about '200 towns, villages and districts were associated with the Hanse'. The constitution was amorphous. An assembly or *Hansetag* met at irregular intervals, which grew longer in the fifteenth century, but it was poorly attended and important towns flouted its rulings (*Rezesse*) without incurring the ultimate penalty of expulsion. The vagueness of organization was, indeed, a strength, for foreign towns and princes found it virtually impossible to pin down the merchants who represented the Hanse abroad to any precise commitments, while they were overawed by the almost limitless resources of the League.

It was because of its healthy economic life that the Hanse flourished. Overseas depots or staples (*Kontore*) were privileged by the local government at Bergen, Bruges, London, and Novgorod. Hanse merchants monopolized the trade of the Baltic coast from the Gulf of Finland to Denmark; they were undisputed in Scandinavia, in north-west Germany, and in the North Sea. Monopolies were normally extorted by the threat of blockade, but on occasion force was used, as in the victorious campaign against Denmark which culminated in the Peace of Stralsund (1369).

Yet this treaty in many respects marked the limit of Hanse expansion. The ever-stronger rulers of England and Flanders proved less easy to cajole in the fifteenth century, while Dutch and English ships challenged German vessels in the North Sea. The Union of Kalmar (1397) which temporarily joined Denmark, Sweden, and Norway under one ruler was a portent that conditions in the North were to be less favourable to Hanse exploitation; so was the union of Poland and a belatedly Christianized Lithuania (1386, below, p. 205), followed as it was in 1410 by the defeat of the Teutonic Knights at Tannenberg and a decline in German influence on the Baltic coast. By the end of the fifteenth century the commercial activity of the Hanse and its political importance were in decline.

In the Alps (as in other mountain areas) feudal controls penetrated with difficulty and were resisted by the hill-dwellers who retained more personal freedom than lowland peasants and in some areas even possessed a formal association for the annual allotment of the upland pasture. Three forest cantons, Uri, Schwyz, and Unterwalden, were well placed to resist the claims of their overlords, the Hapsburgs in Austria, for they commanded the St. Gothard Pass and were privileged by the Hohenstauffen emperors. In 1291 a formal act of alliance or *confederatio* was entered into by the three cantons and the date is traditionally taken to mark the birth of Switzerland.[1]

At Morgarten (1315) and Sempach (1386) Austrian armies were defeated, and to the control of the mountain route between Germany and Italy the Swiss added another source of future wealth—an infantry force which was for long the most formidable military instrument in Europe, for whose services kings were prepared to pay handsomely. The success of the three cantons in maintaining their interests led to an increase in the alliance: three cities, Lucerne, Zurich, and Berne, joined between 1332 and 1353; two rural areas, Glarus and Zug, were annexed in 1352. The addition of towns strained the *confederatio*, but despite severe friction and even civil war, the allies held together and expanded their control southwards towards Italy. By 1500 the cantons and territories accepting their authority formed a solid block between the lakes of Geneva and Constance, and between the Rhine at Basle and the northern tributaries of the Po. Organization was still ill-defined. In most respects each canton was its own master. The charters which were binding on the confederates were essentially negative in tone. But the interest of the confederation as a whole gradually

[1] The three cantons were associated from an earlier date in fact, probably from 1273.

THE TOWNS 171

penetrated *ad hoc* policy and the meetings of delegates from the cantons were regarded by the outside world, if not by the Swiss themselves, as representing a new political unity.

There can be small doubt that the constitutional inventiveness of the Swiss was inspired by their contacts with the thriving communes of thirteenth-century Italy. It is thus proper to place the republican Swiss Confederation within the framework of the urban development in Europe. Yet the formation of the Swiss Confederation and the survival for some centuries of the German Hanse, important as these developments undoubtedly were, must be regarded as among the more modest consequences of the new trading activity and town life we have described.

By 1300 the original structure of feudalism and seignorialism had passed away in the more favoured areas of western Christendom. The feudal relationship had lost its military character and had become a legal framework governing the tenure of land by the noble class. The lord of the manor was a *rentier*, depending no longer on the services and dues of a peasantry tied by servile obligations but on money payments from a peasantry composed to an ever-increasing extent of tenants (above, p. 60). To these changes the revival of commerce had greatly contributed, and we have also noted (above, p. 62) that the early stages of the transition were accomplished with a marked absence of friction.

The later consequences of urban life and commerce for society at large were not so tranquil. The fourteenth and fifteenth centuries witness a steady embitterment in relations between lords and peasants.

On three occasions this flares up into major revolutionary movements: in Flanders (1323–8), northern France (1358), and England (1381)—heralds of similar upheavals in sixteenth-century Germany. Why does this occur? What new factors disturbed the relatively harmonious relationships of earlier days?

The older answer to this problem gave great weight to the Black Death which, most drastically between 1348 and 1350, and only less severely on many later occasions, reduced the population and the wealth of Europe. Carried along the thronged trade routes, it spread with a vicious speed which indicates the degree to which commerce had unified Europe and penetrated into the most remote areas. The depopulation caused by the pestilence was severe enough: in some areas (e.g. Tuscany) as much as three-quarters of the population was struck down, and few places escaped without a loss of a third. But it is now clear that earlier famine, and especially the dearth which affected great parts of Europe between 1315 and 1317, had an almost equally disastrous effect. Indeed, it has been plausibly suggested that the plague was normally preceded by a famine, as it certainly was in Florence, where its onset forms the background to the *Decameron* of Boccaccio (*d*. 1375). The recurrent and widespread famines in Europe in the fourteenth century are also good evidence for contemporary dependence on long-distance commerce.

In short it is evident that the steady expansion of population and of agricultural production had halted towards the end of the thirteenth century. The reason for this may well be the over-exploitation of the new land occupied during earlier 'internal colonization' (above, p. 119). This land was marginal and its productivity was not easily maintained, while the prodigal felling of forests led to soil erosion in some places. Scarcity thus became endemic and when widespread famine followed by plague arrived, they merely intensified an existing contraction in the wealth of Europe, of which they are thus more truly to be considered the consequences than the causes. The frequency of general taxation in the fourteenth and fifteenth centuries enables the drop in population to be measured with some accuracy in surviving records. In Brabant, for instance, the total number of 'hearths' dropped from 92,738 in 1437 to 75,543 in 1496, the contraction being greatest in the smaller towns of the area, where the population dropped by almost two-thirds. Only in certain rural areas—notably in Flanders and in central and northern Italy—does there seem to have been any steady rise in population in the fourteenth and fifteenth centuries. Elsewhere there is a decline revealed in shrinking farms, empty villages, roads and paths overgrown and deserted.

The social consequences were immediate. Prices rose steadily; the labour force dwindled. Lords struggled to maintain their position not merely by foreign adventure and civil war at home (which also did terrible damage to agriculture and the peasantry, below, p. 191), but by stabilizing prices and reverting to labour services at a time when the peasant was already resentful of those that had survived the early period of social amelioration. The example of the 'liberties' of the towns was before the discontented peasantry and it is significant that the three great upheavals mentioned above took place in areas of considerable urban development. In the Flemish rising Bruges and Ypres were, indeed, associated with the rebellious peasants; the 'Jacquerie' of 1358 coincided and was connected with popular disturbances in Paris led by Étienne Marcel; while many Londoners sympathized with the peasants in 1381. Above all there was an egalitarianism in the air which generalized discontent into a political programme in which anti-clericalism had its part. The lords reacted vigorously. The revolts were suppressed brutally and effectively.

Yet the process of change itself the lords could not arrest. If they wished to have labour they had to offer tolerable terms, and so the process which turned the serf into a free peasant continued. But the freedom was essentially a legal freedom. Economically the peasant, no longer possessing a right to his land, was weaker, and the way was paved for progressive landlords to develop their estates as economic units, by enclosure and the cultivation of a staple crop. This was in its turn to influence the status of the landlord. A family was no longer able to survive for centuries on its estates merely by drawing off a minimum subsistence in services or in rent. A new spirit of enterprise made good management important and the proverbial 'ploughboy to ploughboy in three generations' derives from a new social situation where land had to pay its way. The time-table of these changes varied from one part of Europe to another: in general the process is retarded the farther one goes eastwards. There were other variations determined by geography and tradition. All areas did not lend themselves to the capitalist cultivation of specialized crops which wool made possible in England or wheat in Prussia.

The regression in agriculture and the decline in the population as a whole are reflected in the urban activity of the fourteenth and fifteenth centuries. Whether they were dominated by patricians or guildsmen or a body representing both, the old towns pursued restrictive and selfish policies designed in a spirit of purely local protectionism. The Flemish towns, for example, tried to prevent any manufacture of cloth in the adjoining country-side. Rivers and canals passing through towns enabled crippling tolls to be placed by the short-sighted burgesses on goods in transit. This parochial mercantilism hampered long-distance trade, which in any case suffered from the marked decrease in Oriental commerce resulting from the incursions of the Mongols and the expansion of the Ottoman Turks (below, p. 201). The extraordinary advances in commercial technique and the machinery of banking and credit in which Italy had taken the lead might thus have proved sterile if in France, England, and Spain strong monarchies had not controlled urban protectionism in the interests of a larger State, and if the Atlantic and the Pacific had not ultimately replaced the Mediterranean and the Baltic as the channels of mercantile activity.

CHAPTER VII

KINGS AND COUNCILS

Papal sovereignty in theory and practice; secular monarchy; reaction against monarchy; in the Church, the Schism and the Councils; the Hundred Years War; kings and princes emerge supreme; decline and overthrow of the Eastern Empire; the later Crusades.

IN 1302 Boniface VIII issued the bull *Unam Sanctam*[1] with its definition of universal papal sovereignty (above, p. 102). The practical impotence of the papacy should not detract from the importance of the document. If popes were weak, kings were not, and the sovereignty which Boniface had defined became the aim of secular rulers. In the *Defensor Pacis* (1324) of Marsilio of Padua the omnipotence of the civil executive was formally defended by an Italian at Paris University, while the English philosopher Ockham, besides a growing number of Roman lawyers inside and outside Italy, cautiously added fresh arguments to justify the supremacy of princes. The last stage in the theoretical apparatus of monarchy was reached by the mid-fifteenth century when in both Germany and Spain we find the novel notion of the divine right of kings making its appearance.

[1] Papal bulls (above p. 104) are quoted by their opening words.

These speculative doctrines were not, of course, in themselves prime sources of princely power, but its reflection. Theorists defended kings because kings were becoming the masters of their kingdoms.

In the practice of government the papacy provided an object lesson no less valuable than its contribution to political thought. During the two centuries after 1250 the popes were unable adequately to control their Italian dominions and, for seventy years after 1305, were established at Avignon, then just outside the kingdom of France but near enough for them to be occasionally at the mercy of French pressure. But during the fourteenth century the machinery of papal government was extended as never before and, as if to compensate for a declining control over the laity, the grip of the *curia* over the clergy was tightened. For long senior clergy had sought confirmation of their appointments by the pope. Now the pope reserved for his own disposal ever more extensive categories of Church benefices, to which he made provision by nominating clergy who had asked for promotion. Among such 'impetrants' were large numbers of university men, each university forwarding annually to the *curia* a list of those of its graduates[1] for whom provision was requested. The legal work of the *curia* was also greatly extended, not only because of the high reputation of papal courts, but also because papal provisions frequently involved litigation between a candidate to a benefice who had been nominated by the pope and another who had been elected or appointed locally. To deal with the mass of business the papal chancery was progressively enlarged until

[1] And sometimes undergraduates.

it became the biggest and most efficiently organized bureaucracy in Christendom.

An even greater expansion took place in the *camera apostolica* or treasury department, for the collection of taxes from Christendom as a whole became more important as the papacy was divorced from its feudal income in Italy or used this income solely to preserve its control in the Papal States. The *camera* was, significantly, a more important office than the chancery. Provided with its own law officers, elaborate accounting offices, a staff of collectors scattered over the countries of the West, the *camera* was headed by a *camerarius*, or treasurer, who was always more powerful than the vice-chancellor, who was responsible for the secretariat. The *camerarius*, who provided the money for a papal court which proved more and more expensive as it indulged in growing public ostentation, collected Church income from a wide variety of sources. The most important were the 'common services' which prelates paid on their promotion, and 'annates' or the first fruits of benefices, exacted from all clergy who were provided with a living by the pope. These taxes had in effect replaced the older general taxes imposed on the clergy, the tithes originally raised for Crusades. As common services and annates declined in value in the fifteenth century the popes were driven to more dubious ways of raising money, including the sale of offices in the papal court itself.

Every Church institution was by now in complete obedience to the pope. By the fourteenth century it was accepted that only a pope could summon a General Council or validate its decisions; the great religious Orders were, at any rate on paper, amenable

KINGS AND COUNCILS   179

to papal control; the universities were usually loyal allies of the *curia*. From the headquarters of the Church went forth legates to carry papal programmes to the provinces. These legates, described as *a latere* (from the side of the pope), had immense powers delegated to them, and their stately journeys through the length and breadth of Christendom were visible (and expensive) reminders of the grandeur that was Rome.

This administrative development was watched with interest by contemporary kings, whose predecessors had in earlier days found much to copy from the more sophisticated methods of the papal *curia*. By the thirteenth century the gap had if anything widened between papal administration and that of even the most advanced countries in the West. Yet the over-all business of the kings of France or England was to grow with astonishing speed in the fourteenth century and later, while their revenues were vastly greater than that of the Roman Church. These temporal kings had, indeed, more resources than the pope precisely because they had not allowed their feudal income to slip through their fingers. The royal domain, in common with most land, yielded by now money rather than services, but this was sedulously collected by the Crown or the officials to whom it was given in farm. Yet this, the 'ordinary' revenue of the Crown, was insufficient for the needs of an active king and had to be supplemented by 'extraordinary' revenue.

On the collection of 'extraordinary' revenue was to hinge the success of kings in a period when money meant able servants, loyal officials, and soldiers. There were precedents for its collection. The king, like any feudal lord, could call on his vassals for pecuniary aid in a time of crisis; even more ancient perhaps were the harbour and customs duties and a variety of tolls. To these sources kings now added direct taxation. The clergy were compelled to pay a proportion of their income, with or without papal connivance. The laity were taxed by the collection of varying percentages of their estimated property or income. These taxes were voted by assemblies of clergy or magnates, meeting either locally or in larger bodies representing the whole kingdom, and coinciding with, or creating, the bodies known variously as Estates or Cortes or Parliaments. These developments may be briefly illustrated from the history of France.

The reign of Philip IV (the Fair, 1285–1314) is critical in this connexion (cf. above, p. 134). In his reign the power of the Crown was extended in all directions and the limits of France were pressed farther in north and east. Above all the king succeeded in mastering for a time two semi-independent feofs, Gascony held by the English Crown and Flanders for long virtually independent. The warfare involved in this aggressive policy drove Philip to a variety of financial expedients. The clergy were compelled to vote supplies—which provoked a first conflict with Boniface VIII, in which the pope was compelled to withdraw a claim that clergy should not be taxed by secular princes. From 1294 the laity were gathered together to vote *aides*. In 1292 an indirect sales-tax was introduced (the *maltolte*). In addition, the king persecuted the Templars and the Jews, whose assets he confiscated; and he sought immediate relief by debasing the coinage and by borrowing freely from Italian bankers, later repudiating his debts. Philip's successors continued these devices, adding further taxes from time to time: the *gabelle* or salt-tax was introduced in 1341 and became permanent from 1360; the hearth- or property-tax (*fouage*, later called by the more general term *taille*) makes its appearance at about this later date and by the mid-fifteenth century was imposed by the Crown each year.

The financial administration matched in complexity these various sources of income. The 'ordinary' revenue, or 'treasure', was in the hands of four treasurers, the whole country being divided in this respect into four *charges*; the treasurers had below them *receveurs ordinaires*, whose areas corresponded with the administrative divisions of the domain (under *baillis* and *sénéchaux*, above, p. 136). Much of the ordinary income was consumed locally by the needs of the domain and the surplus was not collected centrally but was spent by giving creditors of the crown quittances (*décharges*) to present to a local receiver. The extraordinary revenue was administered by different machinery. Responsibility for *aides* and *tailles* was vested in four 'generals of finance' (*généraux des finances*), the four *charges* reappearing in this connexion as four *généralités*. In the *généralités* the *aides* and *tailles* were assessed by two 'elect' (*élus*) in each *élection* (corresponding usually to a bishopric) and collected by a *receveur des tailles* and a *receveur des aides* who were often the same individual.[1] Finally the salt-tax or *gabelle* was

[1] In certain areas these taxes were assessed and levied by provincial estates: the country was thus divided in this respect into *pays d'élections* and *pays d'états*. The above summary omits many lesser officials and many local variations of practice.

under the control of an official termed a *grenetier*. The generals and the treasurers, normally resident in Paris, formed a sort of permanent economic commission and from about 1450 it seems that an annual budget, or *état général des finances*, was prepared to guide royal policy in getting and spending.

This bureaucratic development, already hinted at by the earlier multiplication of officials on the royal domain (above, p. 134) had its parallels in other spheres of royal activity. The specialization of the *curia regis* (above, p. 135) had in any case gone some way by the beginning of the fourteenth century. Legal work was now concentrated in the *parlement*, which was so busy that from 1308 it was in permanent session, dealing with the litigation of a public (by no means confined to subjects living on the royal domain) which increasingly looked to royal courts, and especially to Paris, for good law. Nearer still to the royal person were the senior members of his household (the *hôtel du roi*) and the offices of Chamberlain and Keeper of the Seals were given usually to the expert and intimate advisers of the prince, who were often non-noble in origin, or drawn from the ranks of the lesser nobility on the royal domain. It was no doubt due to the advice of these professional administrators—among whom were several civil (Roman) lawyers—that Philip IV summoned the meeting of the Estates General in 1302.

In essence the Estates General of that year was an enlarged meeting of the *curia regis*—the clergy, the nobles, and the towns all being present in person or by deputies. Such meetings had occurred earlier, though without the representatives of the towns or

'Third Estate'; similarly the Crown had previously consulted separate meetings representative of the burgesses. The gathering of 1302 united the whole 'community of the realm' in answer to the second challenge of Boniface VIII, who attempted to protect an ex-legate from Philip's wrath by declaring that kings should obey popes. The even bolder claim of the pope in *Unam Sanctam* (above, p. 102) encouraged further demonstrations of French loyalty to the king. A meeting of the Estates General took place in 1303, others again in 1308 and 1314. Under Philip IV's immediate successors the Estates General gradually assumed a regular form. The senior clergy were summoned personally; the lower clergy elected representatives. The nobles whose duty it was to attend a meeting tended to avoid a personal appearance and soon met in regional groups to elect representatives or proxies, in much the same manner as the towns chose their deputies. The Estates General thus composed did not supersede local assemblies and provincial estates, which were still called to authorize taxation (cf. above, p. 181 and note). Though frequently used to vote fresh taxes, they had no right to be consulted in this or any other matter. They were thus primarily used by the Crown in an emergency, when royal propaganda had to be widely disseminated. From 1355 to 1358 an attempt was made, led by a rich Paris merchant, Étienne Marcel, to use the Estates General for a general reform of French administration: this project of the twilight days after the French defeat at Poitiers coincided with a major agrarian upheaval (above, p. 174) and ultimately collapsed with nothing achieved. The Estates General met less and less frequently as the French kings of the fifteenth and later centuries got the better of all opposition.

The developments we have sketched for France had their counterpart in many other areas. Royal centralization and taxation were intensified in the thirteenth and fourteenth centuries; the estates were called, and, while meeting frequently at first, gradually ceased to be effective. Normally strong government invoked the estates as its instrument, though in many German principalities the estates arose in opposition to the prince. Sometimes the estates succeeded for a time in establishing themselves as an integral part of the machinery of government, as the Cortes did in the Spanish kingdoms, achieving a precocious control of taxation, expenditure, and policy.

Only in England, however, did the estates or parliament so develop as to become a permanent and essential element in government. In England there were only two houses—a Lords, where nobles and prelates attended in person; a Commons, where representatives of the towns and of the gentry assembled. This recognition of two great social groups, irrespective of the distinctions preserved elsewhere between clergy and laity[1] and between gentry and burgesses, was one important advantage which parliament possessed in England. Another was the great magnates' acceptance of parliament both as a focal point for expressing their discontents and as a means for controlling the ambitious designs of the monarchy. Doubtless the resilience of parliament must be traced back to the obedience shown by the great

[1] The clergy as a whole met separately in the two convocations of Canterbury and York.

barons to the Norman kings; the royal summons to meetings of the Great Council was in general obeyed in England, in contrast to the independence of the great men in continental kingdoms. Yet this alone would have scarcely led to the survival of parliament had not both king and lords found themselves employing it during the crises of the fourteenth and fifteenth centuries.

These centuries witnessed throughout western Europe a marked reaction to royal aggrandizement, and, just as the popes had offered a pattern for kings to copy, so the Church produced a movement of constitutional reform, which, if it had been successful, might have gone far to inspiring similar movements in the secular States of Europe.

In 1378 occurred the Great Schism of the West. After three-quarters of a century of papal residence in Avignon, Gregory XI returned to Rome and died there. The cardinals met to elect his successor in a tense atmosphere. The Roman citizens were shouting for an Italian pope, though the majority of the cardinals was French. In the event Urban VI was chosen, a Neapolitan prelate thought to be acceptable to the French interest. The new pope turned out to be of unstable temperament, liable to fits of cruel rage and a bitter critic of the cardinals. Repenting of their choice, a number of cardinals withdrew from Rome, disowned Urban and elected a Frenchman as Clement VII. Urban had meanwhile nominated further cardinals and Christendom was divided into two 'obediences'—Rome and Avignon. The Schism was not ended until 1417.

This disruption was mainly due to the curious situation in which the cardinals found themselves by the fourteenth century. They had risen in importance with the pope but, though they elected a pope, while he reigned they were, like all other clergy, completely at his mercy. Their immense prestige was buttressed by great wealth. As a corporation, the College of Cardinals shared a good deal of papal income and individual cardinals were lavishly endowed with fat Church livings to enable them to live in the style of great lords. Yet the pope could pursue policies in which they were not consulted or of which they disapproved; he could feather the nests of his relatives to the impoverishment of the hierarchy; he could not only make a cardinal, he could break one. During the fourteenth century the cardinals more than once tried to limit the power of the bishop of Rome, when they met to elect his successor, by individually swearing in the conclave to accept certain restrictions if elected. Such election 'capitulations' proved fruitless. The more dramatic demonstration of 1378 was even more sterile. With Christendom divided revenue fell, public indignation rose and the cardinals, having tried schism as a threat to papal autocracy, tried to end the schism by any means which would not imperil themselves. In 1409 the cardinals of both obediences met at the Council of Pisa and there elected a pope who failed to command the allegiance of all the supporters of the pontiffs of Avignon[1] and Rome. Thus for a time there were three popes.

These proceedings were in a sense no more than unsavoury disputes within the headquarters of the

[1] By this time the 'Avignon' pope, Benedict XIII, had been abandoned by France and was residing at Peñiscola, in Valencia.

Roman Church. Their real importance lies in their making possible a general reformation of the Church by constitutional means. Earnest Christians were shocked long before 1378 by the worldliness of the clergy, which seemed more pronounced the nearer one got to the top of the hierarchy. But clerical corruption was not only found among cardinals, bishops, and other great prelates. As it was mainly financed by pluralism (the holding of more than one benefice by a single individual) and by taxation of the lower clergy, there was an equally shocking squalor among the illiterate and boorish clerks who alone could be persuaded to perform parish work, at any rate in a large proportion of livings. Convents of men and women were often in a parlous condition. Income from endowments had declined and houses survived either in a ruinous state or by allowing the monks and nuns to retain private property and lead private lives, in which claustration was ignored and discipline sometimes broke down to such an extent that the facetious literature of succeeding centuries found its main source of material in the conduct of monks and nuns.

The notion that a General Council might represent the whole Church more faithfully than a pope had found earlier advocates such as Ockham (above, p. 176). The existence of two and then three competing possessors of the papal plenitude of power made it essential to dispense with the rule that only a pope could summon a council. The need for reform—already producing dangerous popular movements associated with Wycliffe in England and Hus in Bohemia—convinced even conservatives that drastic action was needed. Accordingly the Council of

Constance met in 1414 not merely to end the schism but to prevent another occurring and to reform the Church 'in head and members'.

The ending of the schism was relatively simple. Christendom was weary of its ecclesiastical division. The 'conciliar' pope, John XXIII (who succeeded Alexander V elected at Pisa, above, p. 186), was a ruffian and, in a vain attempt to intimidate the Council, deserted Constance and was deposed. The 'Roman' pope, Gregory XII, voluntarily submitted. The 'Avignon' pope was deprived of the obedience of the Spanish Church. By 1417, therefore, the way was clear to elect an undisputed pope and, in a unique conclave in which the cardinals were joined by representatives of the 'nations' into which the Council was divided for deliberation,[1] Martin V was elevated to the throne of St. Peter.

General reform proved infinitely more difficult. A number of laudable decrees were passed, but on the basic question of papal reservation and provision of benefices opinion was divided. Powerful university delegations favoured the pope's retention of rights from which graduates benefited; the bishops were equally resolved that the old rights of the 'ordinary' should be restored. The power of the pope to appoint and translate prelates was hotly debated, for those prelates present had nearly all been papally appointed or confirmed. Many agreed that the cardinals should be numerically restricted and represent the various provinces of the Church; but there was little agreement on how the college—or indeed the pope—was

---

[1] On the lines of the university nations (above p. 74): at Constance there were at first German, English, Italian, and French nations; the Spanish nation joined later.

to be financially supported, for annates and common services were disliked by all except the numerous and influential members of the *curia* itself. And so with other questions: there was unanimity that drastic action was needed; what form that action should take was disputed. It is symptomatic that, in burning Hus, the Council took one of its few positive steps and thereby provoked a national rising in Bohemia. At first it was accepted that reform should precede the election of a new pope; later a weary Council left reform to be settled after the election; and soon Martin V could virtuously complain that he was ready to reform as soon as the reform commission of the Council presented him with its proposals. Finally the contentious matters were left over for direct settlement between the pope and the various 'nations', and a series of concordats[1] ultimately resulted which, though not without significance in increasing royal power, certainly did not achieve any serious improvement in clerical discipline or morality. It was Jean Gerson (*d.* 1429), the devout chancellor of Paris University and one of the doughtiest reformers at Constance, who urged his sister not to enter a nunnery. It was Ambrogio Traversari (*d.* 1439), famed for his sanctity and scholarship and closely connected with the later Council of Basle, who implored St. Bernardino of Siena (*d.* 1444) on no account to accept a bishopric.

As for the prevention of another schism, the Council took two momentous steps. It laid down that, in the last resort, popes were subject to councils and that councils should meet at regular intervals in

[1] The technical term for a treaty between the pope and a secular State.

future. These decrees (April 1415 and October 1417) were not without their critics and the first in particular was resisted by most of the cardinals. They were, indeed, revolutionary statements. They attempted to reverse a trend towards papal absolutism which begins at the latest in the eleventh century. If they had been honoured by later popes they would have turned papal government from a despotism to what contemporaries called a 'mixed monarchy'; the Church might have given the world a model of the 'constitutional sovereign' centuries before this type of ruler was evolved in secular States. But the 'wind in the world blew on the side of kings'. Martin V 'could not bear to hear the word council'. His successors, from Eugenius IV to the popes of the sixteenth century, were terrified of holding another meeting as truculent—or as constructive—as the assembly at Constance. The terms of the decree laying down regular councils led to a council at Basle in 1431. This, however, was only tolerated by the pope until it had reached a compromise with the Bohemian rebels. Eugenius then withdrew his approval from it and Christendom as a whole was offended because the Basle fathers elected a ridiculous anti-pope (Felix V). It was without provoking criticism that Pius II in 1460 ruled out of order any attempt to appeal from a pope to a General Council. The cause of autocratic monarchy was saved.

Resistance to royal power in the lay kingdoms of the West naturally did not follow quite the same pattern, nor did it usually raise the theoretical issues which were debated at Constance and Basle. Yet the similarities are striking. The magnates wished (like the cardinals) to share in the profits of monarchy and all men of any substance resented royal taxation just as they bitterly resented the parvenu royal advisers—the *marmousets*, as the old nobility called the French king Charles V's advisers ('grotesques' would be a suitable English equivalent). The attempt to put kings into commission was at least made. And, in the end, the kings of Europe, like the popes, emerge victorious.

The magnates of the fourteenth century were, as we have seen (above, p. 173), feeling the economic pinch. Their lands were now sources of money, and economic regression hit them hard. The king, whose rights to occasional taxes and regular customs they had earlier neglected to obstruct, could make ends meet by increasing his public rights. The magnates could pass on taxation to the non-noble population and they tolerated this extension of royal power since they hoped for the pickings—not only in collecting the taxes, but also in remunerative court appointments or royal gifts. No clearer evidence is needed than warfare. Of old the baron had fought for land. Now he fought for money; ransoms and booty become the economic incentives to fourteenth-century war. Even service in the king's army was tolerably remunerated and gave a chance for further gain. The 'Hundred Years War' (1337-1453) between England and France was fought mainly by 'contract armies'; the independent or 'free' company sold its services to the highest bidder and the magnate was paid by the Crown in proportion to the size of his hired following, his 'indentured retinue'.

Possession of royal favour now meant that the lucky magnate could tap the growing wealth of the

Crown. Both in France and England fourteenth-century monarchs gave members of their own family enormous territories as appanages (above, p. 189). This was, of course, to lead to more demands and both Richard II of England and Charles VI of France were surrounded by hungry relatives. Richard's minority and Charles's madness made exploitation relatively simple. Consider the gains of Louis d'Orléans, Charles VI's brother, during the king's periods of sanity (for the duke of Burgundy had more power during the periods of madness): Valois, Touraine, Angoumois, Périgord, Blois were the main territorial gains, while he received nearly a million and a half gold francs at various times and an annual pension of 12,000 gold francs secured on the *aides*.

Besides accumulating internal wealth, princes and the hordes of needy gentry who attached themselves to successful dynasties sought expansion abroad. Charles of Anjou (above, p. 161) had shown the way and a fresh generation of Angevins adventured in southern Italy while the house of Orléans had designs on Milan. Above all, the dukes of Burgundy acquired Flanders, joined the two halves of their patrimony and latterly sought to create a separate principate by extending into Germany. England, an island, lent itself less well to this type of aggrandizement, but the Black Prince in Aquitaine, John of Gaunt in Spain, and Humphrey, duke of Gloucester in Hainault pursued plans similar to those of French princes. Above all, Henry V's victorious campaign in France (Agincourt, 1415) gave English magnates a chance to enjoy the profits of power. When Henry V and Charles VI died in 1422, Henry's brother, the duke

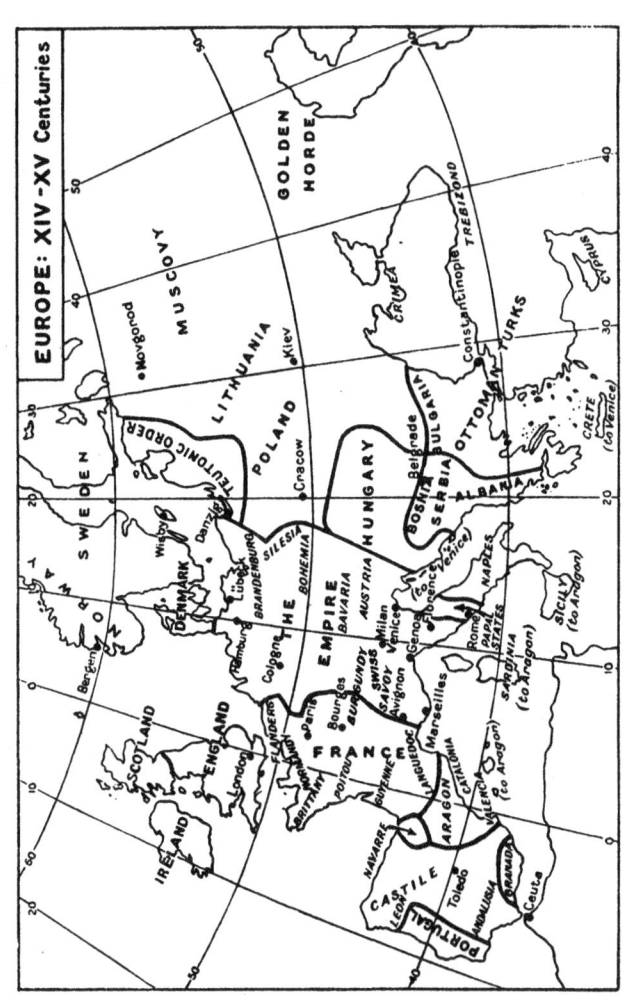

Map II. Europe: XIV–XV Centuries

of Bedford, ruled much of northern France as the regent of the infant Henry VI, heir to both kingdoms, and a whole generation of English barons tasted the fruits of authority and sometimes made fortunes before the English were finally expelled in 1453.

The civil war in France between Burgundians and Armagnacs or Orléanists[1] began with the murder of Louis of Orléans by John of Burgundy in 1407, though the two ducal houses had long struggled to control the feeble king; it was exacerbated by the murder of John of Burgundy by the dauphin's party in 1419. Ambitions as violent characterized the English scene, where three kings (Edward II, Richard II, and Henry VI) were deposed and brutally murdered. English magnates, however, could and did appeal to parliament: the revolutions of 1327 and 1399 were relatively peaceful. Edward III (*d.* 1377) and Henry V (*d.* 1422) appeased baronial discontent by overseas war and foreign conquest; it was only after the loss of France that aristocratic dynasticism in England reached its zenith. 'When the English were back in their own country', wrote Philippe de Commynes (*d.* 1511), the shrewdest political observer of the day, 'none of them wished to reduce his social position: there was not enough property in England to satisfy everyone.'

The most important points to note in the holocaust of civil and foreign war in England and France are: first, that the magnates and their hangers-on sought at no point to destroy monarchy as such, but merely to dominate it; and second, that at the end of the

---

[1] Charles of Orléans (Charles VII, *d.* 1461) married a daughter of Bernard of Armagnac, a southern noble who led the dauphin's faction.

period the kings of France and England emerge stronger, rather than weaker, than their predecessors two centuries earlier. The evidence for this is clear in England, where the Yorkists expropriated the Lancastrians, and the Tudors the Yorkists. In France our best evidence is the use by the discontented magnates of the dauphin Louis as a figurehead in opposition to the re-established rule of Charles VII, the pitiful attempt to cover selfishness by an appeal to the Common Weal made by the great men who fruitlessly resisted Louis XI (d. 1483), the total absence of any genuine Burgundian patriotism even under Charles the Bold—who, like his supporters and French subjects, accepted without question what we may call French 'nationality'. As for the latent power of monarchy, this very element of national consciousness plays its part. Henry V could rely on popular hatred of France among his English subjects. In France, Joan of Arc (d. 1431) canalized French hatred and fear of England. This same fear led the French to accept the expensive luxury of a standing army, the *gens d'ordonnance du roi*, established by Charles VII and maintained by his successors. The great magnates as a class had, indeed, no strength to resist the king. Ransoms and ravaged lands took as big a toll as did death in battle of the older nobility, whose rights had been almost as ancient as those of the ruling dynasties and who were now replaced by a new aristocracy directly dependent on the Crown for its creation and privileges.

Louis XI in France, Henry VII in England had no effective rivals. Masters of their kingdoms, surrounded by able and devoted experts in administration, on good terms with the towns and favourable to commerce (which they manipulated in favour of their political policies and in a growing spirit of mercantilism), they deliberately destroyed the great 'liberties' that interrupted the uniformity of their power. The great appanage duchies which reverted to the Crown proved easily assimilable, for the dukes had tried to copy royal centralization and had their own *chambres des comptes*, estates, and local government officials, all of which could be taken over more or less intact. The greatest 'liberty' of all, the Church, was by this time practically subservient to kings, for the concordats following Constance (above, p. 189) more or less accepted the units of provincial Churches in each kingdom. Kings, as we have seen (above, p. 180) had earlier exercised their power to tax clergymen and to appoint prelates as they saw fit. This practice was now more or less accepted by the pope, who could only hope to share in the spoils. From Louis XI onwards the rights of the 'Gallican' Church were sedulously pressed by French kings. In England monarchs were even more drastic in putting the clergy under the State from Edward III (Statute of Provisors) to Henry VIII (dissolution of the monasteries and royal headship of the Church). Only in England the Crown used parliament to further its autocracy, just as the magnates had earlier used it to limit the Crown, and parliament was shortly to become the mouthpiece of interests divorced from the party in power at the court of the omnipotent sovereign. In France the Estates General offer a pathetic contrast. Seldom called, the separate estates were jealous of one another and incapable of acting either as an instrument of monarchy or as a check upon it. The differences between the two countries are significantly underlined by the reception in France (as elsewhere in continental Europe), but not in England, of the principles of Roman law with their exaltation of princely authority.

France and England offer the most emphatic examples of princely success, but the same development may be found in Spain and Germany. The Spanish kingdoms, which had earlier reconquered all but Granada from the Moors (above, p. 122) had elaborate constitutional arrangements, the Cortes (above, p. 184), but they had a more disturbed history than almost any other part of western Christendom and the nobles were for ever participating in wars between the dynasties or in civil wars over the succession in one kingdom. Yet here, where geography, tradition, and political practice all favoured a narrow particularism, most astonishing transformations took place in the fourteenth and fifteenth centuries. Aragon acquired a vast Mediterranean empire (Balearic Islands, Sicily, Sardinia, Naples, and, for a time, the duchy of Athens); Aragon and Castile were united in the persons of Ferdinand and Isabella (married 1469, inherited both kingdoms by 1479); and Granada was conquered (1492). In close alliance with the towns the Spanish sovereigns could afford to take less notice of the Cortes and depend far more on a strong army and an obedient Church. The hierarchy in the peninsula had always been remarkably obedient to the lay power. The Spanish Church, as reformed by prelates like Cardinal Ximenes, was to become almost a department of State.

In the Empire, as we must still call Germany, the emperor was by the mid-thirteenth century stripped of all real power (above, p. 145). For a time there was no real emperor at all, and when the office was filled again in 1273 there was no question of resuming the earlier attempts at centralized government. Princely integrity at a level below the emperor was ensured by the emergence of a corps of 'electors'—three of the ecclesiastic and four of the secular magnates having the right to fill a vacancy in the empire.[1] Their rights were confirmed in 1338, when it was ruled that the pope had no part in the election of an emperor, and in 1356, when the emperor Charles IV promulgated in the Golden Bull a statement of electoral powers which made them independent of the emperor in law as they had long been in fact. Thus accepted into the German 'constitution' the electoral houses, and following their example, the princes as a whole, set about consolidating their power, making good their control over the lesser nobility and the local prelates, introducing the principles of Roman law to reinforce their authority. The emperor as such had no resources, and took office merely because the dignity had prestige value and enabled its holder to prosecute even more ruthlessly the dynastic policies of his class. During his reign Lewis IV of Bavaria (1314–48) ringed Germany with Wittelsbach lands. His successor, Charles IV (*d.* 1378), was as ardent in the cause of the Luxemburg family, rulers of Bohemia. In the fifteenth century the office became hereditary again in the house of Hapsburg—a step tolerated by the princes because the emperor as such was a figure of no significance. There was, it is true, a constitution. The Reichstag, or imperial assembly, consisted of a

---

[1] The archbishops of Mainz, Cologne, and Trier; the count palatine of the Rhine, the duke of Saxony, the margrave of Brandenburg, and the king of Bohemia.

college of electors, a college of princes and, by the end of the fifteenth century, a few representatives of the Imperial Free Cities. But the deliberations of this body were inconclusive and ineffective, and it consistently jibbed at any step which might have increased the power of the nominal ruler of Germany. Germany was in later days to be united, not under Hapsburg emperors, but under the descendants of Hohenzollern margraves of Brandenburg.

In France, England, Germany, and Spain the sovereign thus emerges as the dominant political authority during the fourteenth and fifteenth centuries, while in Italy the tyrant makes his appearance at the same time (above, pp. 161, 163). There was, however, one monarchy which declined steadily in this period, the empire at Byzantium. The events in the West which we have been considering were not unconnected with the contraction and final collapse of the Eastern Empire.

The Latin Empire of the East lasted for half a century (above, p. 131), during which time the authority of the emperor dwindled and the lands he directly controlled were reduced to narrow strips on either side of the Sea of Marmora, some of the Aegean islands and isolated territories in Thessalonica (Mt. Athos) and the Peloponnese (Mistra). For the rest Frankish magnates dominated the mainland and the Venetians many of the islands, while fragments of Greek rule survived at Trebizond, in Epirus, and at Nicaea. It was from Nicaea that the dynasty of the Palaeologi recaptured Constantinople in 1261, aided by an alliance with the Genoese, rivals in eastern trade of the Venetians. While the Latin Empire did not last long, its consequences were durable and serious. The empire had been weakened beyond recovery; the Palaeologi were utterly dependent on foreign aid, military and commercial; while the Greeks loathed and distrusted the West and all it stood for as a result of the sack of Constantinople in 1204 and the subsequent rapacity of the 'crusaders'.

The emperors of the last Byzantine dynasty were faced with overwhelming problems. The Balkans were passing through a period when the clansmen were temporarily united under heroic kings. Bulgarians in the early thirteenth century, under the Tsar Johannitza (*d.* 1207), had nearly swept the Latins out; in the fourteenth century the Serbs were led by Stephen Dushan (*d.* 1355), who all but captured Constantinople itself. These dramatic incursions into Greek territory were short-lived, but were accompanied by a steadier shift southwards among the Balkan peoples—Albanians moving into Greece and Vlachs into modern Wallachia. The old European provinces of Byzantium were thus primitivized by constant warfare, invasion, and Slav infiltration. The Black Sea area was even further out of control. In the course of the thirteenth century a wave of Mongol or Tartar invasion engulfed both eastern Europe and China. Under Jenghiz Khan (*d.* 1227) and his descendants Russia was invaded and Kiev occupied (1240), the princes of Novgorod surviving as the tributaries of the Golden Horde, a fate which also befell the Seljuk rulers of Asia Minor. From 1279 China was in the power of Khubilai Khan and a Mongol empire had been created which stretched from the sea of Azov to the Pacific. Though their raids were terribly destructive, the unity of Asia and Europe thus accomplished put fresh life for a short time into the overland routes to the East, and both missionaries and merchants followed the path later made famous by the travels of Marco Polo and his uncles (1260, 1271).

More important for the West was the upheaval in the Near East occasioned by the destruction of Seljuk power. This enabled other Turkish tribes in Asia Minor to further their own interests. One such tribe in north-west Anatolia turned against, not its Turkish neighbours, but the easier prize of the Byzantine Empire. It emerged aggressively under its leader Osman[1] (d. 1326) already turning from pastoral activity to war, already converted to Islam. Under his successor, the Sultan Orkhan, the Greek cities south of the Sea of Marmora were all taken, and a domestic war introduced the Ottomans into the Byzantine mainland. John V Palaeologus was virtually Orkhan's vassal when the latter died in 1360. From 1365 Adrianople became the Ottoman capital, Constantinople was effectively cut off from the West except by sea and the Ottomans methodically conquered Macedonia, Thessaly, and Epirus, besides spreading northwards into the Balkans. The only major reverse they encountered was due to the provocation offered by Sultan Bayezid (d. 1403) to the last great Mongol ruler Timurlenk (d. 1405), who destroyed the Ottoman forces in 1402, as he had earlier broken resistance in Persia, Russia, and India.[2] But this check to the Ottomans was temporary: Timurlenk was not interested in Anatolia but swept off towards China, and the Palaeologi were unable to

[1] Or Othman: hence either Ottoman or Osmanli as adjectives.
[2] Marlowe's names, Bajazeth and Tamburlaine, may be more familiar to English readers.

make effective use of their reprieve. After the fall of Constantinople in 1458 the Ottomans inexorably pressed on, reaching Belgrade and the Dalmatian coast by the close of the fifteenth century. Much of their success was due to the employment of Greek generals and Christian soldiers. Their tolerance of the Orthodox rite in return for taxes, their efficiency and even their autocracy, were in a sense congenial to their Greek subjects and vigorous resistance to their advance only came when they reached Croatia and Hungary.

The subjugation of the eastern half of Christendom by a new Moslem power was not regarded with equanimity in the West. True, since 1054 the Greeks had been regarded as schismatics and attempts to heal the schism always foundered on the hatred of the Byzantines for what they regarded as the upstart, pope-ridden, and innovating religion of Rome—a feeling greatly intensified by the arrogant brutality of the Latins in the Levant during the thirteenth century. Political insecurity drove the Palaeologi to submit to the Roman Church in 1274, 1369, and 1439, but on each occasion the Greek Church refused to accept the settlement negotiated by the Greek emperor. Despite these rebuffs the Avignon popes took great interest in schemes to convert the infidel (inspired in part by the evangelical teaching of the Catalan mystic, Ramòn Lull, *d*. 1315), and continued to preach the Crusade. An enormous literature on the recovery of the Holy Land developed during the fourteenth century; the resulting Crusades were fiascos.

The kings of England and France, the princes of Germany and Italy, were absorbed in centralizing policies which also preoccupied the great magnates in a contrary sense. The Church could call crusades, but it was morally weaker than ever, and, divided by schism or distracted by councils, it was powerless to concert resistance to the Ottoman Turk. Moreover it was with difficulty that the Ottoman threat was fully apprehended. Many small expeditions were directed against Egypt and Syria, following the older pattern of the campaigns to save Jerusalem, and the vulnerability of the surviving Greek lands often proved irresistible to western adventurers. A company of Catalan mercenaries ravaged Macedonia and established themselves in the duchy of Athens in 1811, while Rhodes, nominally a Byzantine island, had been captured by the Knights of St. John in 1810. Above all, deadly enmity divided Venice and Genoa. Rivals in Italy, they were even more fiercely estranged by competition for trade in the Aegean and the Crimea. Genoa was entrenched in Galata, a suburb of Constantinople, where the remaining wealth of the Empire was diverted into the pockets of the merchants. Both Genoa and Venice were at first anxious to enter into alliances with the victorious Ottomans, and Venice only fought against the new masters of the Near East (1462–79) in order to secure her trading rights. This is the background against which must be placed the only large-scale campaign organized in the West. The future German emperor, Sigismund, called for support in a drive through the Balkans against Bayezid. A large army of western knights responded and in 1396 they advanced south. At Nicopolis on the Danube they were utterly routed. Sigismund made an ignominious escape by sea, but a large number of the crusaders were captured. Many were slaughtered and the rest the Turks held to ransom for enormous sums.

Sigismund's appeal had been launched when he was king of Hungary. It was the Hungarians alone who, in the fifteenth century, consistently resisted the Ottomans. Hungary had suffered much in the thirteenth century from Mongol invasion and the rivalries of her own backward nobility. In the fourteenth century a degree of order was introduced by kings descended from Charles of Anjou (above, p. 161). In the fifteenth century the Ottomans threatened the continued independence of the land. In the face of the threat, the Hungarians rallied round a soldier, John Hunyadi (*d.* 1456), and his son Matthias Corvinus, who became king (*d.* 1490). Belgrade was relieved in 1456 and the victories of the Hungarians made the Ottomans respect the Danube frontier for a time. The heroic resistance of the Albanians under Skanderbeg collapsed after his death (1468).

Other countries of eastern Europe were in no state to help in this activity. In Poland the nobles had weakened the monarchy by exacting a series of devastating concessions. Bohemia had been roused by the execution of Hus (above, p. 189) to an anti-German movement which rapidly became a social revolution and which, though a settlement was negotiated in 1436, soon flared up again; a reforming noble, George Podiebrad (*d.* 1471) was elected king. The fundamental weakness of monarchy in eastern Europe is betrayed by the bewildering dynastic changes of the fourteenth and fifteenth centuries. The Angevin Lewis, king of Hungary in 1342, became king of Poland also in 1370; Sigismund at different times ruled Hungary and Bohemia as well as the

Empire; Albert of Hungary (1437) became king of Bohemia (1438); Vladislav III of Poland (1434) was metamorphosed into Ladislas V of Hungary (1440). How could rulers whose kingdoms came (and went) so easily offer genuine resistance to the new autocrats at Byzantium?

The decline of the crusade after 1204 was not only a result of the preoccupation of the West with wars between kings and against kings; it was also a cause of such conflicts. In the eleventh and twelfth centuries the magnates could go on crusade relatively simply. Frankish knights had been able to look forward to pious combats and territorial rewards in Syria; later, German knights had flocked to the crusade in the Baltic area. The difficulty of the eastern crusade by the end of the thirteenth century was evident: the Byzantine emperors were too weak to organize the approach to Syria; the Italian maritime republics at the best thought not of reconquest but of ridding the sea of pirates; the Seljuks, and even more the Ottomans, were more than a match in numbers and tactics for the chivalry of the West. The crusade in the North died for different reasons. In 1386 the Lithuanian prince Jagiello married the heiress of Poland, and became Vladislav II of Poland. The Lithuanians, among whom Orthodox Christianity had begun to penetrate from Russia, were now converted to Latin Christianity. The avowed purpose of the Knights of the Teutonic Order was thus removed, and so was an outlet which had absorbed the bellicose energies not only of German knights but also of some French and English nobles as well. Deprived of easy military exercise and the hope of gain in both the north-east and south-east of Europe, is it surprising that the magnates, both great and small, fought so vehemently to control the sources of wealth and prestige at home? Is it surprising that they were interested in the fifteenth-century effort to find across the oceans fresh fields for military and mercantile expansion?

CHAPTER VIII
NEW WORLDS—
ANCIENT AND MODERN

Intellectual and emotional innovations: (a) heresy; (b) Mendicant Orders, Franciscans and Dominicans; (c) Aristotle, Averroism, and Nominalism; northern mysticism; and Italian humanism; concept of the 'middle age'; overseas exploration and the Portuguese; Christendom and Europe.

THE flowering of town life and commerce described in Chapter VI had important consequences not only for economic and political affairs but also for science, sentiment, and religion. One notable development, the university, which has already been touched on (above, p. 74), might well have been discussed as a product of urban society rather than as an aspect of the episcopal school from which it grew. Certainly during the thirteenth, fourteenth, and fifteenth centuries the towns and the universities combined to promote an intellectual ferment such as had not before been seen in the West. The main aspect of this which struck contemporaries was heresy. Virtually unknown in the Latin Church between the eighth and twelfth centuries, heresy was endemic in the West from about 1200. Closely connected again with towns, universities, and heresy, was a novel development in organized religion: the Mendicant Orders, notably the Franciscans and Dominicans, whose members were vowed not only to individual but also to corporate poverty. The link connecting these developments was the new wealth created by commerce.

This we may see by looking at the first popular (as opposed to academic) heresies of the late twelfth and thirteenth centuries. Manichaeism,[1] the acceptance of two irreconcilable principles governing the universe, one good, the other evil, had never been totally extinguished in earlier ages and was associated with the Bogomil sect and Bulgaria.[2] This form of dualism flowered in North Italy and the south of France in the twelfth century. Known as the 'Cathari' (Greek, 'pure') or (in France) as the Albigensians from their centre at Albi, the adherents of this belief opposed an unspotted life of the spirit to a corrupt material existence, and certain elect members, the *perfecti*, adopted a way of renunciation and austerity matching their convictions: flesh-eating, marriage, and property were totally rejected. These relatively few 'perfects' formed the priestly order among the Cathari. There were many simple believers and the 'bourgeoisie and feudality of the Midi adhered *en masse*'. Against this challenge to its control and this criticism of its traditions the Church reacted vigorously, while their rejection of social conventions made an attack on the Albigensians seem legitimate to the French Crown and the nobles of the north of France. A crusade was preached against the heretics by Innocent III in 1208 and a

[1] From Manes or Manichaeus, who lived in Persia, third century A.D.
[2] Hence the pejorative *bougre* of French and its English equivalent.

bitter war followed which increased royal control of Languedoc (above, p. 111) and ultimately exterminated the Cathari.

More orthodox in origin, though sharing with Catharism a rejection of worldly wealth, were other contemporary movements. The Humiliati, or Humble Men, drew their adherents from the cloth-weavers of northern Italian towns, and conflicted with the Church less because they practised a sort of communism than because they attacked the worldly clergy. Peter Waldo was a merchant at Lyons, who abandoned the world and his wealth to found a group of 'Poor men of Lyons'. The Waldensians were evangelical puritans and were vowed to poverty. When condemned by Innocent III they attacked the papacy as anti-Christ.

From the beginning of the thirteenth century onwards, there is an unbroken series of popular movements akin to the Waldensian. The Beguines, Beghards, and Lollards, some of the commoner terms used to describe them, were men and women who accepted a life of poverty: the English word 'beggar' derives from Beghard. Individually or in small loosely organized communities, these members of the laity were thus a living condemnation of both the Church and civil society. As a result they tended to be persecuted by both, though some groups obtained the protection of a local bishop and a few established an accepted 'order', like the Brethren of the Common Life, associated with the book trade and the copyists of manuscripts in the fourteenth century. The Waldensians had worked in the Rhône valley. The Beghards and Lollards were found in England, the Rhineland, and Flanders, and it was in Flanders that the Brethren of the Common Life began their activities. The existence of such groups, and a widely diffused sympathy with their aims, lent explosive force to the evangelism of Wycliffe (*d.* 1384) in England and Hus (*d.* 1415) in Bohemia.

St. Francis of Assisi (*d.* 1226) fits squarely into this movement. The son of a rich Tuscan merchant, Francis underwent a sudden conversion: the perfection he sought was achieved by his marriage to the Lady Poverty and in 1209 he began preaching the total renunciation of worldly wealth. Where St. Francis differed from many other apostles of poverty was in his acceptance of nature and of the Church. He sought out mankind in the mass for his evangelical activities and he obeyed the pope. These two attitudes proved in some respects to be mutually incompatible. While Innocent III gave formal approval to the Friars Minor (friar=brother), he and later popes insisted that the Order should have a formal rule and that the small groups of St. Francis's disciples who worked and begged their way through the Italian towns should be organized. By the time of the saint's death a deep division was growing among his followers. There were those who accepted a hierarchy within the ranks of the Order, with the concomitant wealth of convents[1] and endowments; there were those who clung to the original magic of the master's words—'no friar should have any thing save a robe with a girdle and breeches'.

Unquestionably the Franciscans were the biggest single factor in redeeming the Church in the centuries

---

[1] The related order for women founded by St. Clare was from the start subject in principle to strict claustration, like all orders of women religious.

following 1200 from contempt, for they did much to bridge the gap between laity and clergy and by their preaching reawakened Christian faith in town and country-side. Yet the Order also produced infinite dissension. The 'conventuals' who accepted the rule were bitterly hostile, as was the papacy, to the 'spirituals' who, in the face of persecution, formed small, ascetic communities of *fraticelli*, or 'little brothers', especially in the hills of southern Italy. In the fourteenth century there were fresh troubles when the conventuals divided over the attempt of Pope John XXII to make the order legally responsible for the vast property it had acquired. This schism was theoretical (*de opinione*) as opposed to the earlier schism over the life of apostolic poverty (*de paupere vita*), but it released a flood of speculation of an anti-papal character and in particular inspired the political writings of Ockham (above, p. 187). On top of these feuds, the Grey Friars were bitterly resented by bishops and parish clergy, whose sins they castigated and whose income from alms and burial fees they depleted.

Poverty was also fundamental in the order which took its name from St. Dominic (*d.* 1221). The Order of Preachers was established primarily to combat heresy by means of learned and eloquent sermons. Hence the Order from the start gravitated to the universities and especially to Paris. Hence, when the papacy reorganized the old episcopal responsibility for the intellectual and moral welfare of Christian souls into a regularly established papal inquisition (1233), this was staffed predominantly by Dominicans. The Black Friars were thus never so involved in popular heretical movements, but their connexion with academic speculation had its own temptations. For, at the same time that Peter Waldo and St. Francis were advocating a poverty which cut at the root of the temporal power of the Church, there were intellectual developments on foot which threatened traditional Christian doctrines in more insidious, and, in the long run, more influential ways. The staple ingredients of earlier Christian philosophy had been the Bible and the Latin Fathers, especially St. Augustine, whence had come many Platonic, Neo-Platonic, and Stoic notions (cf. above, p. 22). To this the twelfth century added a much fuller knowledge of the teachings of Aristotle, and an intellectual revolution began which was at first violently resisted by the hierarchy and which was helped on by several Dominican scholars.

Aristotle had been known in the Christian West prior to the twelfth century mainly through the fragments of his work translated by Boethius (above, p. 74). In the Moslem world, however, his writings had long been studied in their entirety, together with other Greek philosophical and scientific texts. The Arabs learned much from the civilizations they conquered (above, p. 34). From Persia and India they acquired astrology and astronomy; from Greece they derived knowledge of medicine, mathematics, and philosophy. Arab scholars were not content to accept the sciences thus obtained, but made them the basis for fresh inquiry. During the eleventh and twelfth centuries the great centres of Arab culture produced many original philosophers and scientists. Among the most important were Avicenna (*d.* 1087) and the Spanish Arab Averroes (*d.* 1198), who based his teaching on a materialist interpretation of

Aristotle. Contact with the Moslem world provided one of the routes by which the West reacquired the full works of Aristotle (as well as other Greek writings). Toledo, recaptured in 1085, was the home of several translators who turned the 'New Aristotle' from Arabic into Latin. Sicily, another recaptured Arab land, also contributed translations. In the thirteenth century fresh translations into Latin were made from the original Greek, as a result of the Latin rule at Constantinople.[1]

It proved an auspicious time for the reception of Aristotle and of his Arab commentators. The earlier synthesis had been well expressed by St. Anselm (*d.* 1109): *credo ut intelligam*, 'I believe in order to understand'; but already in Anselm's own day Berengar of Tours and Roscelin of Compiègne had in practice reversed this approach. In Abelard (*d.* 1142) systematic speculation had a weightier champion, and, though his views were condemned (above, p. 75), the new Scholasticism was ever more eagerly cultivated in the schools and especially at Paris. In the first half of the thirteenth century Aristotle's *Metaphysics* and *Ethics* became available in Latin translations and were immediately popular in the university, despite papal prohibitions which went unheeded. From 1255 the condemned works of Aristotle were formally prescribed by the Paris faculty of Arts. A popular legend developed that Aristotle had on his death been immediately carried up to Heaven.

[1] It should be stressed that the West in these ways acquired and greatly revered many spurious and unworthy books (like the immensely popular and encyclopaedic *Secret of Secrets*, attributed to Aristotle) as well as works of genuine science and scholarship.

This interest in Aristotle was not due to any weakening of the religious impulse. On the contrary, the liveliest teachers sought to show that his doctrine was complementary to the precepts of revealed religion. Many men of learning participated in the task of reconciliation, striving to harmonize Aristotle with the sources of Christian dogma and, above all, with the Bible. This work was accomplished principally by two Dominicans: Albert the Great (*d.* 1280) and St. Thomas Aquinas (*d.* 1274). Though they encountered severe criticism from the hierarchy and later from a rival school of Franciscan theologians, who retained allegiance for the Augustinian tradition, Thomism (as St. Thomas's doctrines were termed by later ages) enjoyed a tremendous vogue. By the fourteenth century the papacy had accepted Aristotle as thoroughly as it had formerly condemned him. This was partly because by the end of the thirteenth century it was possible to distinguish clearly between the Arab commentators, notably Averroes, and what was regarded as the true canon of Aristotle's writings. Averroes, however, had his disciples, and fourteenth-century speculation tended to abandon the delicately adjusted balance worked out by St. Thomas. These two further developments—Averroism and later Scholasticism—were in their different ways to be perhaps of greater significance even than Thomism in the evolution of European thought.

Averroism—which we may loosely take as a materialist philosophy—had its first Latin exponent in Siger de Brabant (*d.* about 1282), who attempted to explore Aristotle's thought, not for its correspondence with revealed truth or faith, but to its logical conclusion, which he found to entail doctrines such as the eternity of the world and the mortality of the soul. Such a position could only be adopted by a Christian if faith and reason were divorced from one another, if a truth in philosophy was not necessarily valid in religion. A doctrine of 'double truth' was, in fact, the principal article brought against Averroists in a series of official condemnations which effectively reduced their influence at Paris by the mid-fourteenth century. Thereafter Averroism found its most important home at the university of Padua, where, under the tolerant control of Venice, a sceptical and scientific tradition gradually grew up in the late fourteenth and fifteenth centuries.

The variety of Nominalism which replaced St. Thomas's form of realism (cf. above, p. 75) as the fashionable philosophy of western universities during the fourteenth century, was not very different from Averroism in that it also tended to involve a divorce between reason and faith. Ockham, in the mid-fourteenth century, and nearly all later masters accepted a gulf between God's infinity and fecundity and the circumscribed speculation of mere men. This, the philosophical *via moderna*, led to a concentration on logical disputation unrelated to theological or moral truth, which was felt to be apprehended by faith rather than by reason. Yet by freeing creation from the shackles of Thomist causation, the Nominalists made possible a far more rational or empirical attitude to natural phenomena, thus producing a further parallel with later Averroism as practised at Padua. Such a 'scientific' approach had, be it noted, already found its theorist in Roger Bacon (*d.* 1292), and, in fact, the Paris

Nominalists of the fourteenth century laid the basis for a new concept of motion.

The scientific revolution of the second half of the seventeenth century had its roots in Paduan Averroism and in the scientific theories of Nominalists like Buridan (*d.* about 1358) and Oresme (*d.* 1382). But at the time the developments we have sketched were more important for the reaction they provoked than for their positive achievements. The reaction on the part of the official Church, though hostile particularly to Averroism, was seldom consistent or effective. There were highly placed Averroists in papal service in the fourteenth and fifteenth centuries, and Nominalism also commended itself since the two arch-heretics of the period, Wycliffe and Hus, were both academic realists of a sort. The reaction which mattered was a spontaneous rejection of both the materialism and the logical subtleties of the schools.

In northern Europe this rejection of Scholasticism took forms which were primarily mystical. It may be seen at work in men like Gerson (above, p. 189) and Nicholas of Cusa (*d.* 1464), highly trained and alive to the most advanced intellectual developments of the day, the one an official of Paris University and the other a cardinal, but alike accepting a lowly and direct contact with religious mystery and humble in their thought. But the reaction is chiefly seen in the long line of mystics stemming from the Dominicans at Strasbourg, and above all from Eckhart (*d.* 1327). This, reinforced by the *nova devotio* of the Brethren of the Common Life (above, p. 209), culminated in the Flemish mystic Thomas à Kempis (*d.* 1471). The *Imitatio Christi* of à Kempis reveals a profound distrust of learned speculation: 'many have lost devotion whilst they sought to search into things too high... human reason is feeble, and may be deceived, but true faith cannot be deceived'.

It is impossible to determine with exactness how deeply this German and Flemish mysticism had taken root, but it is hardly fanciful to see in the emergence of the printing-press direct evidence that there was an insatiable demand for works of devotion. The first book printed with movable type which has survived in its entirety is associated with the names of the inventor Gutenberg, the capitalist Fust, and the type-cutter Schoeffer: it is a Bible printed at Mainz about 1454–6. About 100 editions of Latin Bibles were published in the ensuing fifty years, and many German and Italian translations. Of the *Imitatio Christi* fifteenth-century printers produced no fewer than seventy editions, an average of nearly two issues a year. As printing spread to other countries in northern Europe[1] it maintained its connexion with devotion in general and popular devotion in particular, in this way (as in others) reflecting and intensifying existing cultural tendencies.

In southern Europe the protest against the schoolmen took a significantly different line, though great mystics (like St. Catherine of Siena) are found in fourteenth-century Italy. In this, as in so much else, the stage was set by Petrarch (*d.* 1374), son of a Florentine exile at Avignon. Curious of the world, skilled in Italian poetry and Latin letters, Petrarch found no satisfaction in the contemporary university, and in the Averroists of Padua he discerned enemies

[1] France, 1470; Spain, 1474; England, 1476; Scotland, 1508. The first Italian printing seems to date from 1464.

of literature and therefore of life. In his treatise *On his own ignorance and that of other people*, Petrarch boldly opposed an avowed eclecticism to the worship of the materialist Aristotle, who was 'a great and wise man, but human and therefore fallible'. How much worthier were Plato and Cicero, for both would have been Christians. How much more urgently needed is moral philosophy than this sterile modern science which cuts off knowledge from action, wisdom from virtue! In this work, as in his other writings, Petrarch drew attention to the relevance of the moral teaching of antiquity and, while his invocations of Plato and St. Augustine can be paralleled in the writings of many northern mystics, the emphasis he laid on Cicero was novel and destined to be symptomatic of a profound change in the climate of cultivated opinion in Italy.

Dante (*d.* 1321), in his *Divine Comedy*, where the thought of an earlier period is triumphantly summarized, regarded Cicero as merely one of a group of distinguished pagan thinkers—Plato, Socrates, Avicenna, Averroes, and many more—who surround the 'master of the wise', Aristotle (Inferno IV, 180–144) in Limbo. It is the poet Virgil, prophet of Christ in the Fourth Eclogue, who represents the summit of human achievement and who guides the poet through hell and purgatory to the threshold of heaven. For Petrarch, and for succeeding generations, Cicero played a somewhat similar part, his mastery of prose being a splendid reflection of his luminous mind. 'Eloquence', says Petrarch, 'is nothing other than wisdom flooding forth in words . . . the orator and master of formal beauty must study virtue and wisdom.' The master-teacher of both language and moral values was Cicero, not Virgil. The transformation was, however, due to more than Petrarch's genius. The invitation to consult the ethical experience of Latin antiquity was accepted with alacrity because it provided the justification of a way of life for which traditional Christianity had no place.

Consider the predicament of the prosperous merchant. His fortune was founded upon a careful accumulation of capital. This the Church stigmatized as greed. His business was conducted by borrowing and lending. This the Church described as usury and condemned as both immoral and unnatural. His whole life was one of action, buying and selling, travelling and negotiating, as a citizen running his guild and the government of his town. With this the Church contrasted the solitary life, cloistered calm and chastity. In a word, the man of affairs was concerned with the world and the flesh, and these (said the moralists, though the theologians were more cautious) were connected with the Devil. There was Scriptural authority for the difficulty rich men experienced in entering the Kingdom of Heaven, and Jesus drove the money-changers from the temple. However far the clergy themselves departed from austerity, however much popes employed bankers, canonists connived at usury, or monks and nuns openly enjoyed every comfort that wealth could provide, the precept never changed: 'the love of money is the root of all evil'. One of the commonplaces of popular moral tracts was a debate to decide which was the most vile, the soldier whose hands must needs be bloody or the merchant who could not avoid being covetous. It was, indeed, precisely this element in Christian doctrine which St. Francis had sought to make the basis of his way of life, and the wild success of the early Franciscan movement shows how acutely the townsmen of the thirteenth century sought a release from the burden of their sinful station. The abundant churches and charities of the medieval town testify eloquently to this civic disquiet, and the Franciscan Order itself found it impossible to avoid property and cash, the conscience money of generations of business men. These tensions existed in all urban communities, but were naturally most oppressive in the Tuscan and Lombard areas, where towns entirely dominated the scene.

In the pages of the ancients and especially of Cicero, however, lay a reasoned defence of the life of action, a view of civic responsibility as a noble and public-spirited duty, a doctrine of wealth which made riches a sign of honour and munificence a virtue. Moreover the Italian townsman was, even when living under a tyrant, accustomed to republican forms of government which fitted in with the republicanism of many classical writers and, as an Italian patriot, he enjoyed penetrating a period when the Romans had conquered the world. These are some of the elements in the revival of classical literature in Italy, the Renaissance or rebirth. The energy which was devoted to mastering classical Latin, to recovering as many as possible of the writings of antiquity, to exploring the monuments and emulating the art of Rome and Greece, derived from the emotional actuality of these phenomena, distant in time though they were. They legitimized the present; gave it appropriate form and expression.

It was a process involving much indecision and heart-searching. The most easily assimilated notion was that the Italian might claim the Latins as his kin. Italy had been so long divided politically (above, p. 161) that the longing for unity was general, though perhaps not very profound. In the past the only satisfaction of this emotion had seemed to lie in the realm of government, where the 'Roman' emperor lay to hand in Germany: it was to the emperor that Dante had turned in his treatise *On Monarchy* (c. 1313). During the fourteenth century Italians learned to enjoy the primacy of old Rome, with an added pride in their current superiority in letters and art. The exaltation of Cicero was agreeable to Petrarch, at any rate in part, because it involved a corresponding depreciation of Greek culture as a whole, and not merely of Aristotle. 'Of old the Romans beat the Greeks in battle and the art of war', wrote Piccolomini (below, p. 231), 'now they beat them in every branch of scholarship and learning.' The remaining rivals of modern Italians, the Spaniards, the French, and the Germans, whose political ambitions had for centuries been fed with Italian conquests, were technically referred to by the Roman term 'barbarians'.

Next the Italian bourgeoisie absorbed the republican ideals of Rome. As early as 1347, indeed, an attempt was made under the leadership of Cola di Rienzo, who headed a popular revolution at Rome, to recreate the old hegemony, not of the empire, but of the republic. This proved a chimera, but it was symptomatic of a new appreciation of an epoch in Roman history where there were problems and personalities not dissimilar from those found in the city-states of fourteenth-century Italy, and which had been neglected for a thousand years. As we have observed, the prince was the real power in Italy as elsewhere at this time, but even in the very act of surrendering power into the hands of one man the concepts of republicanism were invoked: the city of Florence was almost completely in the grip of the Medici when the dead Cosimo was honoured by the Ciceronian description *pater patriae*, 'the father of his country'. While many a despot reigned, the reputation of Caesar tended to decline.

The justification of the life of action was more difficult to accept, conflicting as it did with the monastic ideals of the preceding millennium. In the Middle Ages Cicero had been regarded as a woman-hating recluse and Petrarch was horrified when he discovered in the 'letters to Atticus' a Roman citizen who was whole-heartedly committed to the politics of his day, active, ambitious, absorbed by mundane cares. Petrarch could only argue that Cicero had been forced against his will into action, and that his philosophical works had been composed in a solitary old age. It was not till the next generation that the relevance of this side of Cicero was seized upon. Petrarch's pupil, the humanist scholar Salutati (*d.* 1406), who for forty years was chancellor (secretary of State) in Florence, argued that Cicero had participated in politics precisely because he was a wise and virtuous man.. For Leonardo Bruni (*d.* 1444), another Florentine chancellor, Cicero's greatness lay precisely in his double role—the philosopher-man of affairs; and Dante, the supreme Florentine poet and thinker, could now be praised because he combined literature and a full public life, as a soldier, citizen, and father of a family.

The last conquest of ancient values was the defence of wealth, for St. Francis's denunciations were still ringing through Italy, and some of the writers of Rome, like Cicero, were less helpful in this connexion since they frequently stressed the austere simplicity of an earlier and ideal type of Roman citizen as a means of criticizing their own lax days. Though Petrarch, as an old man, had advocated a golden mean in worldly comfort, the prevailing view in the fourteenth century was that true virtue was compatible only with poverty, and a revival of Stoicism helped to keep scholars respectful, at all events in theory, of the Franciscan contempt for wealth. This attitude could scarcely survive the employment of humanist scholars in positions of public importance and honour. By the mid-fifteenth century the chanceries of nearly every Italian city were in the hands of men who could write classical Latin; each dynasty had its humanist historian and writer of official panegyrics; from the pontificate of Nicholas V (*d.* 1455) the papacy itself made the new learning part of the machinery of papal administration and propaganda. Purists might criticize Bruni for accumulating a fortune, but his Florentine colleagues, business and professional men, had nothing but praise for his honestly earned riches, while Bruni himself justified the acquisition of wealth from the pages of Aristotle and Juvenal: only the wealthy man could properly exercise virtue; poverty could distort and demean. From then onwards humanists provided citizens with a reasoned defence of riches: they were not nobler than spiritual things, but the life of the spirit was crippled and frustrated by poverty, while riches enabled the inner life to be translated into works of generosity and beauty. The victory of wealth over poverty was naturally less complete than the other changes in sentiment which have been described. The papal *curia*, for instance, found it hard to accept the idealization of wealth. Whatever the practice of popes and prelates might be, the clergy necessarily remained close to those uncompromising texts in the New Testament which distinguished sharply between the things that were Caesar's and the things that were God's. Yet even in the papal entourage the novel views were upheld. Poggio Bracciolini (*d.* 1459), indefatigable searcher for ancient manuscripts, acute observer of the world around him, imbued with a passion for the new learning which led him to cry 'Cicero is my father', was a papal secretary. In his dialogue *On True Nobility* he distinguished two legitimate forms of nobility—the civic way of honour and wealth, and the Stoic way of austerity. The moral parity of the citizen and the monk was thus asserted, and the dilemma of the medieval merchant was resolved.

These intellectual positions were achieved in Italy first, since the Italian had an accessible source of inspiration in Latin literature. During ensuing centuries the new attitudes were communicated to northern Europe. There, too, had existed the same tensions as in Italy and there, too, the humanist approach to moral philosophy, the stressing of mundane prudence and of civic ideals proved congenial and contagious. But in northern Europe humanist Latin was always a more artificial medium than it had been in Italy, and the widely diffused

NEW WORLDS—ANCIENT AND MODERN 225

popular religious movements we have described (above, p. 209), coloured the 'trans-Alpine Renaissance'. Certainly a Christian element also figures largely in early Italian humanism: Rome for Petrarch was essentially the Rome of St. Peter and one of the glories of Latin was its Christian catholicity. But in the North these very points were often reasons for doubt in the minds of men for whom Latin and Rome were associated with a Church which had lost contact with the liveliest movements of devotion and which appeared primarily as the vehicle of dead tradition. Moreover by the end of the fifteenth century the earlier eclectic approach to the ancient world was dying in Italy itself: the grammars and lexicons were looming over scholarship and soon only Ciceronian Latin was regarded as orthodox; style rather than substance bulked large in the literature of the latter-day Italian humanist.

In one field the growing pedantry proved fruitful. The first generations of humanists consciously and unconsciously emphasized the links between the contemporary world and the ancient world of Greece and Rome. This involved a new and momentous series of historical categories, for time was now divided into three parts, 'ancient' and 'modern' being separated by ten centuries when it was felt that the human spirit had been relatively dormant. In 1469 an Italian scholar described this trough as the 'middle time' (*media tempestas*) and, though the actual phrases 'middle ages' and 'medieval' had to wait another century, the notion they stood for was born. More important still, the study of the 'middle ages' was also begun, for in 1452 Flavio Biondo (*d*. 1463) completed his *Decades*, a history of the West from 472 to 1440, where for the first time the new epoch was treated as an historical unit. With these limits for the 'medieval period' later scholars were for the most part content, though a subsequent stressing of Greek thought led to the adoption of the fall of Constantinople in 1453 as the true beginning of 'modern times', and there has been a more recent tendency to regard the geographical discoveries of the late fifteenth century as marking a new epoch. To these we must now turn.

The countries of the Spanish peninsula had begun to expand overseas in the fourteenth century. The Aragonese empire—in the Balearic Islands, Sicily, and Naples, and the eastern Empire—has already come before us (above, p. 197). The union of the crowns of Aragon and Castile, as well as the conquest of the Moors in Granada, thus naturally paved the way for even more vigorous enterprise. The way in which fortune and power might be extended had been indicated by the Portuguese. The Portuguese had shared in the reconquest of the Spanish mainland from the Moors, the six-hundred-year crusade which left such indelible marks on all the peoples of the peninsula. Facing the Atlantic and cut off from the Mediterranean by the mountains of central Spain, the sailors of Portugal had a natural inclination to explore the western shores of Europe and Africa, their merchants to trade in the commodities of these areas. In the fourteenth and fifteenth centuries there were several influences which made maritime exploration both urgent and attractive.

The Mongol invasion (above, p. 201) tended in the long run to ruin the overland routes to Asia. The

Ottoman Turks made Near Eastern trade increasingly hazardous and expensive. Both these events were also a challenge to Christian sentiment and propagandists urged that the Turk should be attacked from the rear by expeditions reaching the Near East from the south. Moreover it was firmly believed that in Africa or Asia lay a great Christian power with whom alliance could profitably be made, the realm of Prester John, priest-king of many tributary princes (prester = priest). Nearly all educated men believed that the earth was a sphere;[1] but thought that the three great land-linked continents of Africa, Asia, and Europe, were surrounded by a waste of waters. What therefore prevented expeditions sailing direct to Cathay and India?

The explanation seems to be mainly a terror of navigating vast expanses of ocean in the ships and with the instruments which were at first available. The existing charts plotted only the coasts and it was essential for lengthy navigation out of sight of land to be able to calculate latitude. In the course of the fifteenth century Arab skill in this respect was communicated to the West and the altitude of the Pole Star and finally of the sun were used for these calculations. Yet, though all ocean-going ships used the compass (from at least 1300), the quadrant and the astrolabe needed for the calculations of latitude were at first regarded as being somewhat academic: in 1493, on his second trans-Atlantic voyage, Columbus

[1] The Greeks had reached this conclusion and, though some of the early Fathers had seen difficulties in the 'pagan' doctrine if the Antipodes were inhabited (for how could the Gospel have reached this inaccessible area?), it was never seriously questioned by men of science and was certainly a commonplace in cultivated circles from the thirteenth century onwards.

appears to have left his astrolabe behind. Far more important at first than the provision of astronomical information or instruments was the evolution of a ship which could survive the open ocean for long periods, which was manœuvrable and able to take advantage of prevailing winds, and in which sailors, kings, and capitalists could have confidence. This was achieved by adapting the lateen-rig[1] of Arab vessels in the caravel, which later was still further improved by a mixture of both lateen- and square-rigging.

Much of this technical progress was accomplished under the direction of the Portuguese Prince Henry the Navigator (d. 1460). A contemporary chronicler listed Henry's objects as follows: first, a scientific curiosity about the African coast beyond the Canaries; second, an economic motive, to discover if there were Christian peoples in Africa with whom trade could be conducted; third, the strategical desire to define the limits of Moslem power; fourth, a diplomatic interest in finding a Christian power as ally in the crusade; and finally, a hope that the Gospel might be taken farther afield. The mingling of science, commerce, crusade, and evangelism exactly summarizes the various inspirations which led to the astonishing discoveries of the fifteenth-century Portuguese mariners.

Ceuta, opposite Gibraltar, was conquered in 1415. The Madeira Islands were settled in the 1420's. In 1434 Cape Bojador was doubled. The Guinea coast had been reached by 1458 and in the year of Henry's death the Cape Verde Islands had been discovered. Already trade had justified the prince's patronage of

[1] The lateen sail was triangular and suspended by a long yard at a steep angle from the mast.

scientists and sea-captains: from 1448 the Portuguese had a permanent establishment at Arguim (off the Sahara coast), to handle the growing slave trade; gold and exotic animals began to reach the markets of the West, while the sugar-cane and the vine were successfully established in Madeira. Once the commercial profit had been demonstrated in this way, further advances were even more spectacular. The Congo was reached in 1482, in 1487-8 Bartolomeu Dias rounded the Cape of Good Hope and in 1497 Vasco da Gama sailed to India. The direct route to the Orient had been opened.

This steady overseas activity of the Portuguese, which was to make them for long masters of the spice trade, was at the time more influential than the discovery of the new continent of America. This was accomplished by Christopher Columbus (*d*. 1506), a Genoese in the service of Castile who, as is well known, sought a route to India by sailing west, hoping also to discover 'islands and mainlands in the Ocean Sea'—such as the Azores (where the Portuguese had been since early in the fifteenth century) or the legendary Atlantis or Antilla. In 1492 Columbus crossed the Atlantic for the first time and, though he did not realize it, came upon the outlying islands of a new land mass, which was to take its name from the explorer Amerigo Vespucci (*d*. 1512).

Long before the discovery of a vast new world, to which the Gospel could not have been carried, the spiritual content of the term Christendom had been attenuated. With papal power shattered, with kings omnipotent in Church and State, with orthodox Gallicanism growing up as well as the popular heresies practiced by Hussites and Lollards (and all equally redolent of new national sentiment) what genuine meaning had Christendom in the fifteenth century? Many mystics, indeed, were forced to admit the impossibility of regarding the Church here below as one, and made Christian unity a solely spiritual concept, while the conciliarists envisaged a federal structure for the universal Church. Vernacular literature and literacy were gaining at the expense of both Church Latin and the revived classical Latin of the Italian humanists, while the latter, by proclaiming their Latin inheritance, went far to make Christian Rome a mere appendage of Italian civilization. 'Christendom' was now (with the advance of the Ottoman Turks and the discoveries of the explorers) a word with increasingly archaic associations.

What new term could describe the peoples dwelling in what had been called Christendom? For Greeks and Romans the tripartite division of the world into Asia, Africa, and Europe, had geographical but not spiritual meaning: the adjective 'European' was hardly ever used by the ancients. Significantly enough 'European' seems to have been used first in the West by a Spanish chronicler in the eighth century to describe the Franks who defeated the Moslems in 732. But it is not found during the centuries when Christendom (*Christianismus, Chrétienté*) was a living reality: did not Pope Urban at Clermont (above, p. 126) say 'all the world is exile to the Christian, and all the world his country'? From early in the fourteenth century, however, 'Europe' is found more and more frequently in literature. It is often to be met with in Petrarch's pages and it is regularly used by the humanist, Aeneas Sylvius Piccolomini who had travelled widely in it, and wrote discursively of it in his journalistic essays and histories. Yet for Piccolomini, who became pope as Pius II (d. 1464) and tried to defend the West against the Ottoman Turk by organizing a crusade, as for many in succeeding generations, 'Christendom' was still a lively concept. Indeed, it survived the Reformation of the sixteenth century and even the dynastic wars of the seventeenth, sharing with 'Europe' the allegiance of the literate. It was only during the course of the eighteenth century that 'European' finally ousted 'Christian' as the basic term to describe the politically and doctrinally divided societies of the West. That the idea of a single Christian society should have endured so long is perhaps our best evidence for the coherence of the period between the eighth and the fourteenth centuries, and our best introduction to the character of the succeeding age.

SHORT READING LIST

The following list is restricted to fairly accessible books in English and excludes biographies.

1. General histories with bibliographies (in ascending order of complexity): C. W. Previté-Orton, *Outlines of Medieval History*, rev. ed., 1933; Methuen's 'History of Medieval and Modern Europe', volumes by Z. N. Brooke, C. W. Previté-Orton, and W. T. Waugh; C. W. Previté-Orton, *The Shorter Cambridge Medieval History*, 2 vols., 1952; *Cambridge Medieval History*, 8 vols., 1911–1936. A serviceable bibliography is L. J. Paetow, *Guide to the Study of Medieval History*, rev. ed., 1931.
2. General essays on medieval history: H. W. C. Davis, *Medieval Europe*, 1911; C. G. Crump and E. F. Jacob, *Legacy of the Middle Ages*, 1926; H. Pirenne, *History of Europe from the Barbarian Invasions to the Sixteenth Century*, 1939.
3. For chapters 1 and 2: Rostovtseff, *History of the Ancient World*, (vol. ii, Rome), 1927; J. B. Bury, *History of the Later Roman Empire*, 1889; F. W. Wallbank, *Decline of the Roman Empire in the West*, 1946; F. Lot, *The Ending of the Ancient World and the Beginning of the Middle Ages*, 1931; J. M. Wallace-Hadrill, *Barbarian West, 400–1000*, 1952.
4. For chapters 3, 4, and 5: F. L. Ganshof, *Feudalism*, 1952; J. W. Thompson, *Feudal Germany*, 1928; G. Barraclough, *Origins of Modern Germany*, 1946; Joan Evans, *Life in Medieval France*, 1926; C. H. Haskins, *Normans in European History*, 1916; C. Petit-Dutaillis, *Feudal Monarchy in France and England*, 1936; R. Altamira, *History of Spanish Civilization*,

1930; N. Baynes, *Byzantine Empire*, 1925; N. Baynes and H. St. L. B. Moss, *Byzantium*, 1948; Sismondi (trans. and ed. Boulting), *History of the Italian Republics*; P. Villari, *Italy from Charlemagne to Henry VII*, 1910; E. Barker, *The Crusades*, 1923; S. Runciman, *First Crusade*, 1951; H. Waddell, *Wandering Scholars*, 1927; R. L. Poole, *Illustrations of Medieval Thought and Learning*, rev. ed., 1920; C. H. McIlwain, *Growth of Political Thought in the West*, 1932; A. O. Lovejoy, *Great Chain of Being*, 1936; G. G. Coulton, *Five Centuries of Religion*, 4 vols., 1923–50; H. Pirenne, *Social and Economic History of Medieval Europe*, 1936; E. Power, *Medieval People*, 1924; *Cambridge Economic History of Europe*, vol. i, 1941 (agrarian history), vol. ii, 1952 (industry and trade).

5. For chapters 6, 7, and 8: E. Perroy, *Hundred Years War*, 1951; M. Creighton, *History of the Papacy from the Great Schism to the Sack of Rome*, 6 vols., 1897; L. Pastor, *History of the Popes*, vols. i–v, 1891–8; M. V. Clarke, *Medieval City State*, 1926; H. A. Gibbons, *Foundations of the Ottoman Empire*, 1916; J. N. Figgis, *From Gerson to Grotius*, 1907; A. P. d'Entrèves, *Medieval Contribution to Political Thought*, 1939; J. Burckhardt, *Civilization of the Renaissance in Italy*, 1929 (first edition in German, 1860); J. Huizinga, *Waning of the Middle Ages*, 1924; R. de Roover, *Medici Bank*, 1948; (also books in previous list by Barraclough, McIlwain, Coulton, Sismondi).

6. A selection of original authorities available in English translations (for additional material consult C. P. Farrar and A. P. Evans, *Bibliography of English Translations from Medieval Sources*, New York, 1946):
  (a) Collections of Sources: E. F. Henderson, *Select Historical Documents of the Middle Ages*, 1910; R. G. D. Laffan, *Select Documents of European History* (800–1492), 1930; W. E. Lunt, *Papal Revenue in the Middle Ages*, 2 vols., 1934;

SHORT READING LIST 235

L. Thorndike, *University Life and Records in the Middle Ages*, 1944. The preceding books contain mainly public and private documents, as opposed to literary sources of which a good collection will be found in G. G. Coulton, *Life in the Middle Ages*, 4 vols., 1928–30.

(b) Individual works in order of composition or of relevance (details of publication and translator are only given when, so far as I know, there is only one version available):

I CENT. Tacitus, *Germania*.

I–XV CENTS. B. J. Kidd, *Documents Illustrative of the History of the Church*, 3 vols., 1920–41.

V CENT. St. Augustine, *Confessions* and *City of God*.

VI CENT. Boethius, *Consolations of Philosophy*; St. Benedict, *Rule*; Gregory of Tours, *History of the Franks* (trans. Dalton), 2 vols., 1927.

VIII CENT. Venerable Bede, *Ecclesiastical History of the English*.

IX CENT. Einhard, *Life of Charlemagne* (trans. Grant), 1907; Norse sagas—many English versions (cf. W. A. Craigie, *Icelandic Sagas*, 1913).

XI–XII CENTS. *Song of Roland*; *Chronicle of the Cid*.

XII CENT. *Autobiography* of Guibert of Nogent (trans. Bland); Otto of Freisingen, *Two Cities* (trans. Mierow), 1928; *Letters* of Abelard and Heloise; St. Bernard, *On Consideration*, 1908.

XII–XIII CENTS. French romances: many English versions of *Aucassin and Nicolette*, *Tristram and Iseut*, *Romance of the Rose*, *Arthurian Tales*, etc.

XIII CENT. Villehardouin, *Chronicle* (of the Fourth Crusade); *Little Flowers of St. Francis*, *Mirror of Perfection*; Matthew Paris, *Chronicle* (trans. Giles), 1852–4; Joinville, *Chronicle* (of Louis IX); T. Aquinas, *Selected Writings* (ed. d'Arcy), 1939;

Salimbene's *Chronicle* (G. G. Coulton, *From St. Francis to Dante*, 1907); Marco Polo, *Travels*.

XIV CENT. Dante, *Divine Comedy* and *On Monarchy*; G. Villani, *Chronicle* (trans. and ed. Selfe and Wicksteed), 1906; Petrarch, *Secret* (trans. Draper), 1911; Boccaccio, *Decameron*; Froissart, *Chronicles* (trans. Berners, ed. Macaulay), 1895.

XV CENT. Vespasiano da Bisticci, *Lives of Illustrious Men* (trans. Waters), 1926; Platina, *Lives of the Popes*; Commynes, *Memoirs*; N. Machiavelli, *History of Florence*.

INDEX

This is a selective index, but as the text does not attempt chronological surveys of countries and topics, these have been fully indexed.

Abelard, P., 74–5, 213
Agriculture, 42–4, 55–62, 172–4
Albigensians, 111, 139, 208–9
Allodial land, 52, 89, 119, 142, 144–5
America, 35, 229
Anjou, counts of, 50–1, 115–17, 134–5
Arabs, *see* Moslems.
Aragon, 122, 161, 197
Aristotle, 74, 212–14, 218, 223
Arius, Arianism, 11, 17, 23–4
Augustine, St., 8 n., 9–10, 22, 212, 218
Austria, 131, 170
Averroism, 212, 214–18
Avignon, 161, 177, 185–6

Balkans, 9, 21, 124, 200–5
Barbarians, 7, 14–32, 46
Basle, Council of, 189–90
Bayezid, sultan, 201, 203–4
Benedict, St., 13, 64
Bernard, St., 67–8, 75
Bible, Latin, 75, 214, 217
Black Death, 172
Blois, counts of, 112–13
Boethius, 22, 74, 100, 212
Bohemia, 131, 187, 189–90, 204–5
Bohemond, 128–9, 149
Boniface VIII, pope, 102–4, 176, 180, 183
Bourgeoisie, 152–60
Brethren of the Common Life, 209–10, 216

Bruges, 150, 156, 158–60, 169, 174
Bruni, L., 222–3
Bulgaria, Bulgars, 124, 200
Burgundy, dukes of, 192–5
Byzantium, *see* Empire.

Canons, Regular, 68
Capetians, 50, 86–8, 134–40
Cardinals, 97–8, 185–6, 188
Carolingians, 31–3, 83–4, 86–8
Carthusian Order, 68
Castile, 122, 197
Charlemagne, emperor, 32–4, 83–4, 87–90, 121, 131
Charles Martel, 31, 34
Charles VII, k. of France, 194–5
Charles of Anjou, 161, 192
Chivalry, 71–2
Church, Celtic, 24; Greek, 24–5, 127, 202; Roman, 9–13, 23–8, 63–77, 90–108, 141, 177–9, 185–90, 196, 202–3, 207–12, 219–25
Cicero, 218–25
Citeaux, Cistercian Order, 42, 67–8
Clergy, *see* Church.
Clermont, Council of, 114, 126–7
Clovis, 20, 23, 29–30
Cluny, Order of, 66–7, 93, 121
Cologne, 64–5, 150, 156, 158
Colonization, internal, 42, 60–1, 118–20, 172–3

237

Commerce, 3–4, 61–2, 124, 146–53, 159–60, 196, 226–9
Constance, Council of, 188–90
Constantine, emperor, 5, 7, 10–11, 16; Donation of, 95, 101, 103
Constantinople, 5, 16–17, 26, 34–5, 125, 129, 131, 149, 200–2, 213, 226
Crusades, 105, 111, 120–31, 132–3, 139–40, 146, 149, 202–4

Dante, 218, 221–3
Dominic, St., and Order of, 211–14

Education, 73–4, 212–16
Empire, Eastern, 5, 7–8, 16–18, 20–1, 24–5, 34–5, 46, 58, 82, 105–6, 128–31, 148, 199–202; Roman, 3–13, 46, 79–80, 82; Western, 32–3, 83–4, 90, 96–9, 103, 127, 141–6, 161–2, 197–9, 221
England, 30, 35, 46, 52–3, 55, 74, 86, 102, 117, 119, 133–4, 139–40, 150, 154–5, 158–60, 168–9, 172, 174–5, 179, 184–5, 187, 191–7, 209–10
Estates, 140–1, 180, 182–5, 196–7
Europe, European, 1, 230–1
Excommunication, 106–7
Exploration, 200–1, 226–9

Feudal relations, 45–6, 63–6, 77, 84, 125, 130, 137, 140, 142–6, 171
Flanders, 150–1, 155–6, 158–9, 168–9, 172–3, 175, 209–10
Florence, 149, 157–9, 165, 175, 222

France, 29–37, 45–55, 66–8, 73–4, 86–8, 102, 111–18, 133–40, 150–1, 154–5, 160, 172, 175, 177, 179–84, 191–7, 208–9
Francis, St., and Order of, 210–11, 223
Franks, 19–23, 29–33, 83–4
Frederick I, emperor, 103, 132, 143–6, 162
Frederick II, emperor, 103, 144–5, 161, 167
Friars, 210–12.

Gaul, 8–9, 18–19, 23, 29–33
Gelasius I, pope, 27, 103
Genoa, Genoese, 130, 149, 160, 165, 199–200, 203
German tribes, 14, 17–33, 46, 80–2
Germany, 35–6, 45, 52, 55, 64, 88–90, 98–9, 114, 117, 119–20, 131–3, 141–6, 150–1, 156, 166–72, 194, 197–9
Greece, 199–201, 203
Gregory I, pope, 27–8
Gregory VII, pope, 70, 98–9, 101–3, 123

Hamburg, 64, 150, 168
Hanseatic League, 168–9
Hapsburgs, 170, 198–9
Henry III, emperor, 90, 96–7, 132
Henry IV, emperor, 98–9
Henry V, k. of England, 192–5
Henry the Lion, 132, 144–5
Henry the Navigator, 228–9
Heresy, 25, 105, 207–15
Hohenstauffen, 88, 142–6
Holy Land, 121, 125–6, 129–31

INDEX 239

Hungary, 36, 132, 161, 202, 204–5
Huns, 17–18, 20
Hus, J., 187, 189–90, 210, 216

Iconoclasm, 25
Industry, 158–9
Innocent III, pope, 102–5, 161, 208–10
Investiture contest, 98–100
Islam, see Moslem.
Italy, 2–3, 18–29, 31–2, 74, 89–90, 94–6, 98–9, 128, 143–4, 148–9, 155, 157–8, 161–6, 170, 172–3, 177, 192, 217–26

Jerusalem, 26, 121, 126, 129–30
Jews, 9, 71, 129 n., 136, 180
Joinville, J., 70, 137, 146
Justinian, 7–8, 16, 20–1, 23, 75

Kempis, T. à, 216–17
Kingship, barbarian, 28–33; feudal, 47–8, 52–3, 81–90, 133–46; in fourteenth and fifteenth centuries, 176, 179–85, 190–9
Kinship, 84–5
Knightly class, 46–55, 59–62, 69–70, 72, 77, 85, 110–22, 171–4, 191–4

Lateran Council, Fourth, 104–5
Latin, ecclesiastical, 13, 72–7; humanist, 224–5, 230; see Romance languages.
Law, Canon, 75, 95, 97; Customary, 57, 80–1, 84; Roman, 7–8, 75, 80–1, 83, 176, 182, 197–8

Liége, 92, 150, 156
Literature, see Scholarship.
Lithuania, 132, 169, 205
Lombards, 21–3, 32, 136, 160
Louis VI, k. of France, 135–6, 138
Louis IX, k. of France, 70, 136–40, 146
Louis XI, k. of France, 195–6

Magyars, 36, 88; see Hungary.
Manorial organization, 44–5, 55–62, 174–5
Medici, 165, 222
Merovingians, 29–31
Milan, 98, 162–4
Military Orders, 130, 132, 205
Ministeriales, 51, 114, 143
Mohammed, 33–4
Monasticism, 12–13, 66–8, 91–3, 187
Money, 3, 44, 61–2, 115, 137, 148
Mongols, 175, 200–1, 226
Moslems (Arab), 14, 33–5, 121–2, 148–9, 212–13; see Seljuks, Ottomans.
Mysticism, 216–17

Naples, 99, 128, 148, 161, 197
Nobility, see Knightly class.
Normandy and Normans, 46, 53, 88, 116–17, 123, 126
Norsemen, 14, 35–7, 149–50

Ockham, W., 176, 187, 211, 215
Odoacer, 19–20
Open fields, 42–3, 56–7
Ostrogoths, 17–20, 23
Otto I, emperor, 21, 36, 89–90, 131
Ottomans, 175, 201–5, 227

Palaeologi, 199–202
Papacy, 26–8, 90, 94–108, 126–7, 141, 144, 161, 176–9, 185–90, 223
Paris, 74, 134, 150, 174, 213–15
Parliament, *see* Estates.
Peace and Truce of God, 60, 127–8
Peasants, 40–4, 55–62, 171–4
Persia, 18, 21, 25, 84, 124, 125
Petrarch, 217–25
Philip II, k. of France, 102, 136, 138–40
Philip IV, k. of France, 180, 182
Pilgrimage, 120–1
Pius II, pope, 190, 221, 231
Poland, 132, 169, 204–6
Political thought, 100–3, 106–8, 176–7, 190
Population, 40–1, 172–3
Portugal, 122, 226–9
Printing, 217

Renaissance, 220–6
Romance languages and culture, 8–9, 22, 79–80
Rome, 2, 5–6, 19, 26, 32, 96, 120, 162, 185
Russia, 17, 35, 124, 132, 200–1

Scandinavia, 149–50, 168–9
Schism, of East and West, 127, 202; of the West, 185–90
Scholarship and literature, 8, 22, 72–7, 212–26
Seljuks, 125–31

Serfs, *see* Peasants.
Sicily, 34, 128, 133–4, 144, 161, 197, 213
Sigismund, emperor, 203–4
Slavery, 2, 4, 6, 58–9, 71, 229
Slavs, 14, 17, 21, 58–9, 200–5
Spain, 8–9, 18–22, 32, 34, 45–6, 121–2, 141, 160, 176, 184, 197, 212–13, 226–9
Swiss, Switzerland, 44, 169–71

Taxation, 173, 178, 180–4
Teutonic Order, 132, 169, 205
Thomas of Aquinas, St., 214
Tithe, 62, 65
Towns and Town-life, 2, 16, 40, 54, 61, 90, 138, 147–75, 207–11, 219–24

Universities, 74–5, 212–16
Urban II, pope, 114, 126–7, 230
Usury, 4, 136, 219

Vandals, 18–20, 26
Venice, 130–1, 148–9, 157–8, 160, 165–6, 199–200, 203, 215
Vernaculars, 72–3, 77, 230
Virgil, 8, 218–19
Visconti, 162–3
Visigoths, 17–22, 30

Waldo, P., 209
Wycliffe, J., 187, 210, 216

For Product Safety Concerns and Information please contact our EU representative GPSR@taylorandfrancis.com
Taylor & Francis Verlag GmbH, Kaufingerstraße 24, 80331 München, Germany

www.ingramcontent.com/pod-product-compliance
Lightning Source LLC
Chambersburg PA
CBHW071825300426
44116CB00009B/1440